COURAGE TO POSSESS

21 DAY MARRIAGE & DESTINY FAST 2024

Table of Contents

Stay Connected

Weekly Programs:

Midnight Oil Prayers: Monday through Thursday 11:59 pm - 1:00 am EST.
Midday Prayers: Monday through Thursday 11:59 am - 1:00 pm EST.
Bible Studies: Every Wednesday at 7:00 pm EST.
Tarry Night: Every Wednesday immediately following Bible Studies
Friday Fire Night: Every Friday at 7:00 pm EST.
Sunday Service: Every Sunday at 10:00 am EST.

Kingdom Full Tabernacle Locations:

KFT Darien - Headquarters
65 Tokeneke Road
Darien, CT 06820

KFT North Carolina
8600 Crown Crescent Court
Charlotte, NC 28227

KFT Maryland
11000 Mattaponi Road
Upper Marlboro, MD 20772

KFT Dallas
605 E Palace Parkway B4,
Grand Prairie, TX 75050

If you feel led to sow, you can sow via the following platforms:

Zelle: finance@kftchurch.com | Text to Pay: Text "give" to (844)285-9541 | Give tab via www.kftchurch.com | Paypal: paypal.me/oseiministries

Connect With Us:

Instagram: Apostle Dominic Osei - @domosei | Prophetess Lesley Osei - @lesley.osei |
Our Church - @kingdomfulltabernacle | @kingdomfulltabernacle_nc |
@kingdomfulltabernacle_md | @kingdomfulltabernacle_dallas
YouTube: Kingdom Full Tabernacle | Facebook: Kingdom Full Tabernacle

For any questions or concerns, email us at info@kftchurch.com
Share your testimonies at testimony@kftchurch.com
Visit our website at www.kftchurch.com

Welcome to Kingdom Full Tabernacle International Ministries' 21-Day Marriage and Destiny Fast! Beloved, it is with great joy and expectation that we embark on this 21-day spiritual journey together.

Our theme this year is "Courage to Possess." Over the next three weeks, we will seek the face of God, aligning our hearts with His Word, as we strive to strengthen our marriages, unlock our destinies, and claim the promises He has given us.

Let's first take a moment to reflect on what it means to have courage and to possess. According to the dictionary, courage is the ability to do something that frightens you or the strength to persevere in the face of difficulty. Biblically, courage is often described as confidence and trust in God despite fear or uncertainty. As Joshua 1:9 says, "*Have I not commanded you? Be strong and courageous. Do not be afraid; do not be discouraged, for the Lord your God will be with you wherever you go.*" Courage, in this context, is not the absence of fear, but rather, the decision to move forward in faith, knowing that God is with us.

Possessing, on the other hand, means to take hold of, or claim something that belongs to you. In a spiritual sense, it means to claim the promises God has already made available to us. Deuteronomy 1:8 says, "See, I have set the land before you. Go in and possess the land which the Lord swore to give to your fathers." Possession requires action, faith, and persistence. It is not passive; it is about stepping forward boldly, knowing that God has already paved the way for you.

During this fast, we will be praying four times a day—at 12:00 AM, 5:00 AM, 12:00 PM, and 6:00 PM. These times have been carefully chosen to provide you with constant spiritual nourishment throughout the day and night. Each prayer session will cover topics relevant to our lives—whether it's marriage, family, finances, or personal growth. Each of us are walking a unique path, but God's Word speaks to every situation, and His promises are sure.

We encourage you to stay consistent throughout this fast. Fasting can sometimes be challenging, especially as we confront distractions, physical discomfort, or spiritual resistance. However, Galatians 6:9 reminds us, "Let us not become weary in doing good, for at the proper time we will reap a harvest if we do not give up." If you feel weary or discouraged at any point, remember that this fast is a spiritual battleground where victories are won through perseverance. God will honor your sacrifice, your dedication, and your courage to stand firm.

In this fast, we are not just seeking temporary breakthroughs but lasting transformation. We believe that God will give us the strength to walk into the fullness of our destinies and the grace to build marriages and relationships that reflect His love. As you fast, trust that God is at work even in the moments when you feel tired or when progress seems slow. He is faithful, and His Word will not return void (Isaiah 55:11).

As we journey together, let's continually lift each other up in prayer. We are not doing this alone—we are a family united in Christ, pressing forward for a common goal. Expect miracles, breakthroughs, and most of all, expect God to do exceedingly and abundantly above all we can ask or think (Ephesians 3:20).

May God give you the courage to possess all that He has promised. Let's enter this fast with our hearts fully committed to the Lord, knowing that victory is already ours through Christ Jesus.

God bless you!

Praying effectively involves more than just reciting words; it's about building a genuine connection with God, being sincere, and aligning with His will.

Here are some steps on how to pray effectively:

1. Approach God with Humility and Reverence
- **Acknowledge God's Greatness:** Begin by recognizing who God is—His power, holiness, and majesty. When you approach Him with awe and humility, it sets the tone for effective prayer.
- **Scripture Reference:** "Humble yourselves before the Lord, and He will lift you up" (James 4:10).

"Heavenly Father, I come before You in humility, acknowledging that You are holy and worthy of all praise. I stand in awe of Your greatness and love."

2. Start with Thanksgiving and Praise
- **Thank God for His Blessings:** Begin your prayer by thanking God for what He has done and praising Him for who He is. Gratitude opens the heart and strengthens faith.
- **Scripture Reference:** "Enter His gates with thanksgiving and His courts with praise; give thanks to Him and praise His name" (Psalm 100:4).

"Lord, I thank You for Your grace, mercy, and provision in my life. You are always faithful, and I bless Your holy name.

3. Be Honest and Transparent
- **Speak from the Heart:** Effective prayer is sincere and honest. Share your true feelings, struggles, and desires with God. He knows everything already, but He values your openness.
- **Scripture Reference:** "The Lord is near to all who call on Him, to all who call on Him in truth" (Psalm 145:18).

4. Pray According to God's Will

- **Seek God's Will First:** Effective prayer is not just about presenting our desires but aligning with God's will. Ask for His guidance and for the strength to follow His plan.
- **Scripture Reference:** "This is the confidence we have in approaching God: that if we ask anything according to His will, He hears us" (1 John 5:14).

"Lord, let Your will be done in my life. I submit my plans and desires to You, trusting that Your ways are higher and better."

5. Use Scripture in Prayer

- **Pray God's Word:** The Bible is filled with promises and truths that we can pray back to God. This not only deepens your faith but also aligns your prayers with His Word.
- **Scripture Reference:** "For the word of God is alive and active"
- (Hebrews 4:12).

"Lord, You said in Your Word that You will never leave me nor forsake me (Deuteronomy 31:6). *I trust in Your presence and faithfulness today.*

6. Pray with Faith and Expectation

- **Believe in God's Power:** Approach God with faith, believing that He can and will answer your prayers according to His perfect will.
- **Scripture Reference:** "And whatever you ask in prayer, you will receive, if you have faith" (Matthew 21:22).

"Father, I believe that You are able to do exceedingly more than I ask or imagine. I trust that You are working all things together for my good."

7. Be Persistent in Prayer

- **Pray Without Giving Up**: Consistency in prayer shows your dependence on God and your faith in His timing. Don't get discouraged if answers don't come immediately.
- **Scripture Reference:** "Pray without ceasing" (1 Thessalonians 5:17).

"Lord, even when I don't see results right away, help me to trust Your timing and keep praying in faith."

8. Confess and Repent of Sin

- **Seek Forgiveness:** Sin can block the effectiveness of your prayers. Confess your sins, and ask for God's mercy and forgiveness. This brings you back into right standing with Him.
- **Scripture Reference:** "If we confess our sins, He is faithful and just to forgive us our sins and to cleanse us from all unrighteousness" (1 John 1:9).

"Lord, I repent of my sins, and I ask for Your forgiveness. Cleanse my heart and help me to walk in righteousness."

9. Pray in the Spirit

- **Allow the Holy Spirit to Guide You**: The Holy Spirit can help you pray when you don't know what to say. Be open to His guidance, and allow Him to lead your prayers.
- **Scripture Reference:** "The Spirit helps us in our weakness...the Spirit Himself intercedes for us with groanings too deep for words" (Romans 8:26).

"Holy Spirit, guide my prayers and intercede on my behalf. Help me to pray in line with God's will."

10. Close with Trust and Surrender

- **Leave it in God's Hands:** After presenting your requests to God, trust that He will answer in His time and His way. Surrender your burdens and trust Him to work things out.
- **Scripture Reference:** "Cast all your anxiety on Him because He cares for you" (1 Peter 5:7).

"Lord, I place my burdens at Your feet, trusting that You are in control. I surrender all to You and believe that Your will is perfect."

Additional Tips for Effective Prayer:

- Create a quiet space where you can focus on God.
- Set a regular time for prayer, building consistency.
- Pray with others in agreement, as communal prayer is powerful.
- Keep a prayer journal to track prayers and God's answers.

Remember, effective prayer is not about the length or eloquence of your words, but the sincerity of your heart and the alignment of your will with God's. Keep seeking Him in faith and trust that He hears you.

Preparing for the Marriage and Destiny Fast

As you prepare for this transformative 21-day journey, here are a few important steps to ensure you are physically, spiritually, and mentally ready:

1. Set Your Intentions

- Begin by seeking God's direction for what you hope to achieve during this fast. Ask the Holy Spirit to guide your focus. Whether you are seeking breakthrough in your marriage, clarity in your destiny, healing, or spiritual growth, write down your goals. This will give you something to focus on in prayer as you fast and help remind you of why you began.

2. Meal Prep

- Decide what type of fast you wish to do. We often encourage midnight to 6pm fasting and or dry fasting, pending your capability and strength.

3. Prepare Physically

- Choose Your Fast: Decide how you will fast—whether it is a complete fast (abstaining from food), a partial fast (e.g., Daniel fast), or fasting certain meals or types of food. Be sure to select a method that you can maintain and one that honors your health.
- Ease into the fast: If you're fasting food, try cutting down on caffeine, processed foods, or sugar a few days before the fast to avoid withdrawal symptoms.
- Stay Hydrated: Drink plenty of water throughout the fast, especially if you are abstaining from food.

Preparing for the Marriage and Destiny Fast

4. Prepare Mentally and Emotionally
- ○ Expect Challenges: Fasting can be tough, especially in the early days when your body and mind are adjusting. Stay mentally prepared to face distractions, temptations, and possible fatigue. (Refer to Longsuffering Messages on KFT's Youtube Page)!
- ○ Create a Quiet Space: Prepare a designated space for prayer and reflection—a place where you can be still before God. This will help you stay focused and undistracted during your prayer times.

5. Plan Your Prayer Times
- ○ Commit to attending the four daily prayer sessions: 12:00 AM, 5:00 AM, 12:00 PM, and 6:00 PM. Set reminders on your phone or calendar to ensure you don't miss any of these powerful times of connection with God and the church family.
- ○ Use these prayer times to press into God's presence. Don't just pray for what you need, but also listen for what God is saying to you. He may give you specific guidance for your marriage, destiny, and personal life.

6. Limit Distractions
- ○ Consider limiting social media, television, or any other distractions during this time to focus more on prayer and seeking God's voice. Fasting is about tuning out the world to hear God more clearly.
- ○ If possible, set aside times each day to meditate on the Word of God, journal your reflections, or worship. This will help you stay grounded and connected throughout the fast.

7. Build a Support System

- Partner with someone else who is fasting. Share your goals, challenges, and encouragement with them. Having an accountability partner can help keep you on track.
- Stay connected with the church community. Whether it's through the prayer times, online groups, or in person. Knowing you are not alone in this fast will keep you motivated.

8. Prepare for Breakthrough

- Approach this fast with expectation! Remember that fasting, when combined with prayer, is a powerful tool that opens doors and breaks strongholds. As Matthew 17:21 reminds us, "This kind can come out only by prayer and fasting." Believe that God will move in your situation and that breakthroughs are coming, both in your marriage and destiny.

Finally, go into this fast knowing that it is a spiritual battle, but one you will win with God's strength. Philippians 4:13 declares, "I can do all things through Christ who strengthens me." Stay committed, be patient with yourself, and lean on God's grace to carry you through. He will reward your faithfulness!

God bless you as you prepare!

Spiritual Preparation

Spiritual Preparation is extremely Important:

1. Set Your Intentions
Begin by seeking God's direction for what you hope to achieve during this fast. Ask the Holy Spirit to guide your focus. Whether you are seeking breakthrough in your marriage, clarity in your destiny, healing, or spiritual growth, write down your goals. This will give you something to focus on in prayer as you fast and help remind you of why you began.

2. Prepare Spiritually
- Pray beforehand: Before the fast begins, spend time in prayer asking God for strength, grace, and endurance. Psalm 51:10 says, "Create in me a pure heart, O God, and renew a steadfast spirit within me." Ask Him to prepare your heart for this journey.
- Read Scriptures: Begin studying relevant scriptures about courage, faith, and the promises of God. Scriptures like Joshua 1:9, Deuteronomy 1:8, and Galatians 6:9 will be anchors for you throughout the fast.

3. Dreams and Vision Journals for your own Safe Keeping
- During this fast, God may speak to you through His Word, so have your Bible handy. Study scriptures that align with the theme of courage and possessing God's promises.
- Keep a journal nearby to record insights, revelations, and prayers. Writing things down can also help you stay focused and committed to the process. It will allow you to refer back, connect the dots, remember and keep you in hope and awe of God. Remember God reveals, its up to us to be sensitive enough to listen.

Day 1: A Red Sea of Thanks

Thanksgiving is a great way to reflect on all the blessings in your life and give thanks to God. One meaningful way to do this is through prayer. Expressing gratitude through prayer has many benefits. It shifts your focus off negative things and reminds you of God's faithfulness. It can inspire you to live with more joy and it strengthens your relationship with the Lord as you meditate on His steadfast love.

(Psalm 100, Colossians 3:15-17, and 1 Chronicles 16:8-36, 1 Thessalonians 5:18)

Prayer Points:
1. Father Lord, we thank You for Your eternal love that never fails us. (Jeremiah 31:3)

2. O Lord, we praise You for being our refuge and strength, an ever-present help in times of trouble. (Psalm 46:1)

3. Father, thank You for the gift of life and the breath in our lungs. (Genesis 2:7)

4. We are grateful for Your mercies that are new every morning. (Lamentations 3:22-23)

5. Heavenly Father, we thank You for providing for our daily needs. (Matthew 6:11)

A Red Sea Thanks:

Anchor Scriptures: (Exodus 15:1-2, Psalm 100, Colossians 3:15-17, 1 Chronicles 16:8-36, 1 Thessalonians 5:18)

Prayer Points:
1. Father Lord, we thank You for Your eternal love that never fails us. (Jeremiah 31:3)
2. O Lord, we praise You for being our refuge and strength, an ever-present help in times of trouble. (Psalm 46:1)
3. Father, thank You for the gift of life and the breath in our lungs. (Genesis 2:7)
4. We are grateful for Your mercies that are new every morning. (Lamentations 3:22-23)
5. Heavenly Father, we thank You for providing for our daily needs. (Matthew 6:11)
6. O Lord God, we praise You for being the source of all good things in our lives. (James 1:17)
7. Father, we thank You for Your provision, even in times of scarcity. (Philippians 4:19)
8. Lord, we thank You for the gift of family and friends. (Proverbs 17:17).
9. Father, thank You, for the relationships that enrich our lives. (Ecclesiastes 4:9-12)
10. Father, we praise You for the gift of marriage and the blessings it brings. (Genesis 2:24).
11. O Lord God, we are grateful for Your healing power, both physical and emotional. (Jeremiah 17:14)

12. Father Lord, we thank You for the ability to overcome challenges and grow stronger. (James 1:2-4)

13. Heavenly Father, we thank You for the gift of salvation through Your Son, Jesus Christ. (Ephesians 2:8-9)

14. Thank You, Lord, for the peace that surpasses all understanding. (Philippians 4:7)

15. Heavenly Father, we thank You for the gift of salvation through Your Son, Jesus Christ. (Ephesians 2:8-9)

16. Thank You, Lord, for the peace that surpasses all understanding. (Philippians 4:7)

17. We are grateful for the indwelling of the Holy Spirit, our Comforter and Guide. (John 14:16-17)

18. Lord, we thank You for the assurance that Your plans for us are good. (Jeremiah 29:11)

19. Father God, we praise You for the promises You have fulfilled in our lives. (Joshua 21:45)

Day 1: Bartimaeus' Cry

1. Prayer for Mercy and Forgiveness of Sin

Prayer: Heavenly Father, I come before You, acknowledging my sins and shortcomings. I ask for Your mercy and forgiveness. Cleanse me with Your blood, Lord, and create in me a pure heart.
Scripture: *"If we confess our sins, He is faithful and just to forgive us our sins and to cleanse us from all unrighteousness."* (1 John 1:9)

2. Prayer for God's Mercy in Times of Failure

Prayer: Lord, I ask for Your mercy in the areas where I have failed. Help me to rise again, and let Your mercy strengthen me to overcome all my weaknesses.
Scripture: *"The Lord is gracious and full of compassion, slow to anger, and great in mercy."* (Psalm 145:8)

3. Prayer for Restoration through God's Mercy

Prayer: Father, restore to me the joy of my salvation through Your mercy. Where I have lost my way, bring me back to Your path. Restore my heart, mind, and spirit.
Scripture: *"Restore to me the joy of Your salvation, and uphold me by Your generous Spirit."* (Psalm 51:12)

4. Prayer for Mercy in Difficult Situations

Prayer: Lord, I need Your mercy in this difficult time. I cry out to You for deliverance, trusting that Your mercy will make a way for me where there seems to be no way.
Scripture: *"Let Your mercy, O Lord, be upon us, just as we hope in You."* (Psalm 33:22)

5. Prayer for Mercy Over My Family

Prayer: O Lord, I lift up my family to You, asking for Your mercy to cover us. Forgive our mistakes and draw us closer to You. Let Your grace and protection be upon every member of my family.
Scripture: *"The steadfast love of the Lord never ceases; His mercies never come to an end; they are new every morning; great is Your faithfulness."* (Lamentations 3:22-23)

6. Prayer for Forgiveness of Hidden Sins

Prayer: Father, forgive me for the sins I have committed knowingly and unknowingly. Search my heart and reveal anything that is not pleasing to You. I repent of all my hidden faults.
Scripture: *"Who can discern their own errors? Forgive my hidden faults."* (Psalm 19:12)

7. Prayer for God's Mercy to Overcome Temptation

Prayer: Lord, I seek Your mercy to strengthen me in the face of temptation. Help me resist sin and live according to Your will. Let Your mercy guide me and keep me from falling.
Scripture: *"No temptation has overtaken you except what is common to mankind. And God is faithful; He will not let you be tempted beyond what you can bear. But when you are tempted, He will also provide a way out so that you can endure it."* (1 Corinthians 10:13)

8. Prayer for Mercy in Healing

Prayer: Father, I ask for Your mercy to bring healing to my body, mind, and soul. Heal me from every infirmity and forgive any sin that may have caused this sickness. I trust in Your healing mercy.
Scripture: *"Have mercy on me, Lord, for I am faint; heal me, Lord, for my bones are in agony."* (Psalm 6:2)

9. Prayer for Mercy for the Nation

Prayer: Lord, have mercy on our nation. Forgive us for turning away from You. Heal our land, and let Your mercy flow over the leaders and the people, guiding us back to righteousness.

Scripture: *"If My people, who are called by My name, will humble themselves and pray and seek My face and turn from their wicked ways, then I will hear from heaven, and I will forgive their sin and will heal their land."* (2 Chronicles 7:14)

10. Prayer for God's Unfailing Mercy

Prayer: Lord, I trust in Your unfailing mercy. No matter what I face, I know that Your mercy is everlasting and Your forgiveness is complete. Let Your mercy sustain me each day.

Scripture: *"But because of His great love for us, God, who is rich in mercy, made us alive with Christ even when we were dead in transgressions—it is by grace you have been saved."* (Ephesians 2:4-5)

Day 2: Pentecost Pour

Expectation of the Supernatural: Expecting signs, wonders, and prophetic gifts to be released in greater measure as the Holy Spirit moves. A Pentecost Pour revelation often ties into the idea of revival, where the Holy Spirit renews individuals, churches, or even entire regions.

Anchor Scriptures: (Acts 21:4, Acts 4:31, Acts 2:14-15, Acts 9:17-18, Acts 8:14-17, Ezekiel 2:2, Judges 6:34)

1. Prayer for the Filling of the Holy Spirit

Prayer: Heavenly Father, I ask that You fill me with the power of Your Holy Spirit. Let Your Spirit dwell in me, guiding me in all that I do.
Scripture: *"Do not get drunk on wine, which leads to debauchery. Instead, be filled with the Spirit."* (Ephesians 5:18)

2. Prayer for the Spirit of Wisdom and Revelation

Prayer: Lord, I ask for the Spirit of wisdom and revelation to rest upon me. Open the eyes of my heart so that I may know You more deeply and understand Your will for my life.
Scripture: *"I keep asking that the God of our Lord Jesus Christ, the glorious Father, may give you the Spirit of wisdom and revelation, so that you may know Him better."* (Ephesians 1:17)

3. Prayer for Empowerment to Witness

Prayer: Holy Spirit, empower me to be a bold witness for Christ. Let Your power work through me to share the gospel and bring many to salvation.
Scripture: *"But you will receive power when the Holy Spirit comes on you; and you will be My witnesses in Jerusalem, and in all Judea and Samaria, and to the ends of the earth."* (Acts 1:8)

4. Prayer for the Gifts of the Holy Spirit

Prayer: Lord, I pray for the manifestation of the gifts of the Holy Spirit in my life. Let Your gifts of wisdom, healing, prophecy, and discernment flow through me for Your glory.
Scripture: *"Now to each one the manifestation of the Spirit is given for the common good."* (1 Corinthians 12:7)

5. Prayer for Strength and Boldness

Prayer: Holy Spirit, grant me supernatural strength and boldness to face challenges with faith and courage. Empower me to overcome fear and stand firm in Your truth.
Scripture: *"For the Spirit God gave us does not make us timid, but gives us power, love and self-discipline."* (2 Timothy 1:7)

6. Prayer for Guidance by the Holy Spirit

Prayer: Lord, I ask for the Holy Spirit to guide me in all my decisions. Lead me in the paths of righteousness and help me to discern Your will in every situation.
Scripture: *"But when He, the Spirit of truth, comes, He will guide you into all the truth. He will not speak on His own; He will speak only what He hears, and He will tell you what is yet to come."* (John 16:13)

7. Prayer for the Fruit of the Spirit

Prayer: Holy Spirit, let Your fruit manifest in my life. Help me to grow in love, joy, peace, patience, kindness, goodness, faithfulness, gentleness, and self-control.
Scripture: *"But the fruit of the Spirit is love, joy, peace, forbearance, kindness, goodness, faithfulness, gentleness and self-control."* (Galatians 5:22-23)

8. Prayer for the Spirit's Empowerment in Prayer

Prayer: Holy Spirit, empower me in prayer. Help me to pray according to God's will and intercede with groanings too deep for words when I don't know how to pray.
Scripture: *"In the same way, the Spirit helps us in our weakness. We do not know what we ought to pray for, but the Spirit Himself intercedes for us through wordless groans."* (Romans 8:26)

9. Prayer for a Spirit-Led Life

Prayer: Lord, I surrender to the leading of the Holy Spirit in every area of my life. Let Your Spirit direct my thoughts, actions, and decisions, so that I may live in alignment with Your purposes.
Scripture: *"Since we live by the Spirit, let us keep in step with the Spirit."* (Galatians 5:25)

10. Prayer for Spiritual Authority and Power

Prayer: Father, empower me with spiritual authority through the Holy Spirit. Let me walk in Your power, overcoming the enemy and advancing Your kingdom with boldness.
Scripture: *"I have given you authority to trample on snakes and scorpions and to overcome all the power of the enemy; nothing will harm you."* (Luke 10:19)

11. Prayer for Revival and Spiritual Awakening

Prayer: Holy Spirit, let there be a fresh outpouring of Your power in my life, my church, and my community. Let revival come, and stir hearts to return to You with passion and purpose.
Scripture: *"Will You not revive us again, that Your people may rejoice in You?"* (Psalm 85:6)

12. Prayer for the Holy Spirit to Reveal God's Purpose

Prayer: Holy Spirit, reveal God's purpose for my life. Let me know the plans You have for me and empower me to walk in the fullness of Your calling.
Scripture: *"For I know the plans I have for you, declares the Lord, plans to prosper you and not to harm you, plans to give you hope and a future."* (Jeremiah 29:11)

13. Prayer for Renewal and Refreshing by the Holy Spirit

Prayer: Lord, I pray for a fresh renewal by the Holy Spirit. Restore my strength, revive my passion, and renew my mind with Your presence and power.
Scripture: *"He saved us through the washing of rebirth and renewal by the Holy Spirit."* (Titus 3:5)

14. Prayer for Spirit-Led Evangelism

Prayer: Holy Spirit, empower me to share the gospel effectively. Give me the boldness and wisdom to witness and bring people into the knowledge of Christ.
Scripture: *"For the Spirit God gave us does not make us timid, but gives us power, love and self-discipline."* (2 Timothy 1:7)

15. Prayer for Spiritual Breakthrough

Prayer: Holy Spirit, break every chain and bring a supernatural breakthrough in my life. Let Your power flow through me, breaking every limitation, and releasing Your blessings.
Scripture: *"Not by might nor by power, but by My Spirit,' says the Lord Almighty."* (Zechariah 4:6)

Day 2: Flame Cleaning

Flame cleaning is a process in which a gas flame is used to remove contaminants, rust, paint, or other substances from the surface of materials, typically metal. The symbolic power of fire for refining, purifying, and removing impurities—parallels to what flame cleaning achieves in the natural realm. Pray that The Lord should sanctify and purify us.

1. Prayer for Purification by Fire

Prayer: Heavenly Father, I ask for the fire of the Holy Spirit to purify my heart and life. Burn away every sin, every impurity, and everything that does not reflect You. Refine me and make me a vessel worthy of Your use.
Scripture: *"He will sit as a refiner and purifier of silver; He will purify the Levites and refine them like gold and silver."* (Malachi 3:3)

2. Prayer for the Fire of the Holy Spirit to Empower

Prayer: Lord, baptize me with the fire of Your Spirit. Empower me to walk in Your boldness and strength to proclaim Your Word and fulfill Your will in my life.
Scripture: *"But you will receive power when the Holy Spirit comes on you; and you will be My witnesses in Jerusalem, and in all Judea and Samaria, and to the ends of the earth."* (Acts 1:8)

3. Prayer for a Zeal and Passion for God

Prayer: Father, ignite in me a burning passion and zeal for Your Kingdom. Let the fire of the Holy Spirit stir up a deep desire to seek You with all my heart and to serve You fervently.
Scripture: *"Never be lacking in zeal, but keep your spiritual fervor, serving the Lord."* (Romans 12:11)

4. Prayer for Spiritual Revival and Fresh Fire

Prayer: Lord, send fresh fire into my spirit. Let the fire of revival burn within me and cause a spiritual awakening in every area of my life. Stir up a hunger for Your presence like never before.
Scripture: *"Will You not revive us again, that Your people may rejoice in You?"* (Psalm 85:6)

5. Prayer for Refining and Transformation

Prayer: Father, let Your refining fire transform me. Remove every hindrance, every doubt, and every fear that holds me back from living in full alignment with Your will.
Scripture: *"Create in me a pure heart, O God, and renew a steadfast spirit within me."* (Psalm 51:10)

6. Prayer for Strength and Courage to Face Fear

Prayer: Lord, give me the strength and courage to face the things that frighten me. Empower me with boldness to confront fear and to walk in the victory that You have given me.
Scripture: *"Be strong and courageous. Do not be afraid or terrified because of them, for the Lord your God goes with you; He will never leave you nor forsake you."* (Deuteronomy 31:6)

7.Prayer to Overcome Fear of the Unknown

Prayer: Father, I place my trust in You for the unknown. I refuse to let the fear of the future control me. I know that You are in control of every situation, and I rest in the assurance of Your plans for my life.
Scripture: *"So do not fear, for I am with you; do not be dismayed, for I am your God. I will strengthen you and help you; I will uphold you with My righteous right hand."* (Isaiah 41:10)

8. Prayer for Holiness and Sanctification

Prayer: Heavenly Father, baptize me with Your holy fire that sanctifies and cleanses me. Help me to live a life of holiness, completely set apart for Your purpose.
Scripture: *"But just as He who called you is holy, so be holy in all you do; for it is written: 'Be holy, because I am holy.'"* (1 Peter 1:15-16)

9. Prayer for Boldness in the Face of Opposition

Prayer: Lord, as You fill me with Your Spirit, grant me boldness to stand firm in the face of opposition. Let Your fire give me the courage to proclaim Your truth, no matter the cost.
Scripture: *"Now, Lord, consider their threats and enable Your servants to speak Your word with great boldness."* (Acts 4:29)

10. Prayer for a Deeper Relationship with God

Prayer: Lord, let Your fire draw me into a deeper relationship with You. Baptize me afresh with the Holy Spirit, and let my desire for intimacy with You grow stronger each day.
Scripture: *"As the deer pants for streams of water, so my soul pants for You, my God."* (Psalm 42:1)

11. Prayer for Spiritual Awakening

Prayer: Father, send Your fire to awaken me spiritually. Open my eyes to see what You are doing in this season, and awaken my spirit to discern Your plans and purposes.
Scripture: *"Wake up, sleeper, rise from the dead, and Christ will shine on you."* (Ephesians 5:14)

12. Prayer for the Fire of God's Love

Prayer: Lord, baptize me with the fire of Your love. Let Your love consume me, filling me with compassion and grace toward others as I reflect Your heart in everything I do.

Scripture: *"For our God is a consuming fire."* (Hebrews 12:29)

Day 3: Deliverance from Fear

When God called Gideon to save Israel from the Midianites, he was afraid and insecure about his ability to fulfill this mission. He initially doubted that God was really with him and asked for multiple signs to confirm God's will.
(Judges 6:36-40).

Prayer: In the name of Jesus, I declare victory over every enemy that has risen against me through evil altars. I stand in the authority of Christ and command all demonic forces to flee.
Scripture: *"Behold, I give you the authority to trample on serpents and scorpions, and over all the power of the enemy, and nothing shall by any means hurt you."* (Luke 10:19)

1. Prayer for Deliverance from All Fear

Prayer: Heavenly Father, I come before You seeking deliverance from every form of fear that has gripped my heart. I reject and renounce fear, and I declare that it has no place in my life because I trust in You.
Scripture: *"I sought the Lord, and He answered me; He delivered me from all my fears."* (Psalm 34:4)

2. Prayer for Faith to Replace Fear

Prayer: Lord, I ask that You increase my faith so that I may overcome fear. Help me to focus on Your promises instead of the circumstances that cause fear in my heart.
Scripture: *"When I am afraid, I put my trust in You."* (Psalm 56:3)

3. Prayer for Deliverance from the Spirit of Fear

Prayer: Father, I break free from every spirit of fear that seeks to hold me captive. I declare that fear is not from You, and I embrace the spirit of power, love, and a sound mind that You have given me.
Scripture: "For God has not given us a spirit of fear, but of power and of love and of a sound mind." (2 Timothy 1:7)

4. Prayer for God's Peace in the Face of Fear

Prayer: Lord Jesus, I ask for Your peace to fill my heart and mind. Let Your peace replace every anxious thought and every fear, as I rest in Your presence and Your promises.
Scripture: *"Peace I leave with you; My peace I give to you. I do not give to you as the world gives. Do not let your hearts be troubled and do not be afraid."* (John 14:27)

5. Prayer for Protection from Fearful Thoughts

Prayer: Father, guard my mind against fearful thoughts and anxious imaginations. Let Your Word be my shield and fortress and protection.
Scripture: *"You will keep in perfect peace those whose minds are steadfast, because they trust in You."* (Isaiah 26:3)

6. Prayer for Boldness and Power through Fire Baptism

Prayer: Lord, baptize me with the Holy Spirit and fire. Empower me to be bold and unashamed in proclaiming the Gospel and in standing firm in my faith.
Scripture: *"For God has not given us a spirit of fear, but of power and of love and of a sound mind."* (2 Timothy 1:7)

7. Prayer for Spiritual Gifts to Be Stirred

Prayer: Father, let the fire of the Holy Spirit stir up every spiritual gift You have placed within me. Let me walk in the fullness of the gifts of prophecy, healing, discernment, and more for the edification of Your church.
Scripture: *"Therefore I remind you to stir up the gift of God which is in you through the laying on of my hands."* (2 Timothy 1:6)

8. Prayer Against the Fear of Failure

Prayer: Lord, I reject the fear of failure in every area of my life. Help me to trust that Your strength is made perfect in my weakness, and You will enable me to succeed according to Your will.
Scripture: *"I can do all things through Christ who strengthens me."*
(Philippians 4:13)

9. Prayer for Deliverance from Fear of Death

Prayer: Father, I reject the fear of death, for I know that Jesus has conquered the grave. I live with the assurance of eternal life and the hope that nothing can separate me from Your love.
Scripture: *"Even though I walk through the valley of the shadow of death, I will fear no evil, for You are with me; Your rod and Your staff, they comfort me."*
(Psalm 23:4)

10. Prayer for God's Love to Cast Out Fear

Prayer: Lord, let Your perfect love fill my heart and cast out every fear. Remind me daily that I am loved by You, and because of Your love, I have no reason to fear.

11. Prayer for Deliverance from Fear of Failure

Prayer: Father, help me to trust You in all things. Deliver me from the fear of failure and help me to rely on Your strength, knowing that I can do all things through Christ who empowers me.
Scripture: *"For I can do everything through Christ, who gives me strength."*
(Philippians 4:13)

12. Prayer to Break Free from the Fear of People

Prayer: "Lord, I renounce the fear of man that has held me captive. Help me to focus on pleasing You above all others, and give me boldness to walk in Your truth, regardless of the opinions of others."

Scripture: *"The fear of man brings a snare, but whoever trusts in the Lord shall be safe."* (Proverbs 29:25)

13. Prayer for Confidence in God's Power

Prayer: "Father, remind me of Your power and sovereignty. Let me have confidence in Your ability to deliver me from all fear, and may I walk boldly, knowing that You are my strength."

Scripture: *"The Lord is my light and my salvation; whom shall I fear? The Lord is the strength of my life; of whom shall I be afraid?"* (Psalm 27:1)

14. Prayer for Protection from Fear

Prayer: "Lord, I ask for Your divine protection from fear. Place a hedge of protection around me, and let Your peace guard my heart and mind at all times."

Scripture: *"The angel of the Lord encamps around those who fear Him, and He delivers them."* (Psalm 34:7)

15. Prayer for Trust in God's Faithfulness

Prayer: "Father, deliver me from fear by reminding me of Your faithfulness. Help me to trust that You are always with me, and that Your plans for me are good."

Scripture: *"The Lord is faithful, and He will strengthen you and protect you from the evil one."* (2 Thessalonians 3:3)

Day 4: Prison of Lack

Lack and poverty are not just physical conditions but can be spiritual strongholds that must be addressed through targeted warfare prayers. In the Bible, we see evidence that poverty and lack can have spiritual roots, including generational curses, demonic spirits, and strongholds that travel through bloodlines, affecting families over generations. These prayers are designed to take vengeance against the spirit of lack and poverty by standing on the promises of God and breaking generational curses.

1. Prayer to Bind the Spirit of Lack and Poverty

Prayer:
Heavenly Father, in the name of Jesus, I take authority over every spirit of lack and poverty that has been operating in my life. Your Word declares that poverty can creep upon a person like a thief, but I stand today and bind every thief that has come to rob me of my financial blessings, spiritual growth, and abundance. By the authority of Jesus Christ, I bind the spirit of poverty and lack and I command it to be cast into the abyss. Every demonic assignment against my life in the area of finances, I break it now in Jesus' name! I declare that I am no longer a slave to lack and poverty, but I walk in divine abundance. Amen.
Scripture: *"And poverty will come on you like a thief and scarcity like an armed man."* (Proverbs 6:11)
"Truly I tell you, whatever you bind on earth will be bound in heaven, and whatever you loose on earth will be loosed in heaven." (Matthew 18:18)

2. Prayer for Breaking Generational Curses of Poverty

Prayer: Lord Jesus, You have redeemed me from every curse by becoming a curse for me on the cross. Therefore, today, I stand on the blood of Jesus and break every generational curse of poverty, lack, and financial struggle in my family line. I declare that every ancestral covenant or pattern of poverty that has been passed down from my forefathers is broken in Jesus' name! Father, I ask that You uproot every seed of lack that has taken root in my bloodline, and by the power of the Holy Spirit, I receive the blessing of Abraham over my life, family, and future generations. Amen.

Scripture: *"I, the Lord your God, am a jealous God, punishing the children for the sin of the parents to the third and fourth generation of those who hate me."* (Exodus 20:5)

Prayer: Lord Jesus, You have redeemed me from every curse by becoming a curse for me on the cross. Therefore, today, I stand on the blood of Jesus and break every generational curse of poverty, lack, and financial struggle in my family line. I declare that every ancestral covenant or pattern of poverty that has been passed down from my forefathers is broken in Jesus' name! Father, I ask that You uproot every seed of lack that has taken root in my bloodline, and by the power of the Holy Spirit, I receive the blessing of Abraham over my life, family, and future generations. Amen.

Scripture: *"Christ redeemed us from the curse of the law by becoming a curse for us... so that in Christ Jesus the blessing of Abraham might come to the Gentiles."* (Galatians 3:13-14)

3. Prayer for Divine Vengeance Against the Spirit of Lack

Prayer: Righteous Judge, I cry out to You today for divine vengeance against the spirit of lack that has attacked my life. Your Word declares that You hate robbery and injustice, and that You will repay those who have stolen from Your children. Father, I ask that You take vengeance against every demonic power that has stolen my financial inheritance, peace, and blessings. Let every altar that has been raised against my prosperity be destroyed by the fire of the Holy Ghost! Every plan of the enemy to keep me in a cycle of lack and scarcity, I cancel it now in the name of Jesus. Let the sword of the Lord bring justice and restoration into every area of my life. Amen.

Scripture: *"For I, the Lord, love justice; I hate robbery and wrongdoing. In my faithfulness I will reward my people and make an everlasting covenant with them."* *(Isaiah 61:8)*

"Do not take revenge, my dear friends, but leave room for God's wrath, for it is written: 'It is mine to avenge; I will repay,' says the Lord." (Romans 12:19)

4. Prayer for Restoring What the Locust Has Eaten

Prayer: Father, I stand on Your promise in Joel 2:25 that You will restore the years that the locust has eaten. Every loss, every stolen opportunity, and every wasted year due to the prison of lack, I ask for supernatural restoration in Jesus' name. Lord, I declare that You are giving me the ability to produce wealth, and I receive the covenant of prosperity You have made with Your people. Restore what was lost to me and let my hands be blessed to create and multiply wealth. Amen.

Scripture: *"I will repay you for the years the locusts have eaten—the great locust and the young locust, the other locusts and the locust swarm."* (Joel 2:25)

"But remember the Lord your God, for it is he who gives you the ability to produce wealth, and so confirms his covenant, which he swore to your ancestors." (Deuteronomy 8:18)

5. Prayer for Deliverance from the Spirit of Slavery to Debt

Prayer: Heavenly Father, I renounce every spirit of slavery that has come upon me through debt. Your Word says that the borrower is a slave to the lender, but I stand in the authority of Christ, knowing that I am no longer a slave to debt, fear, or lack. I declare that I am a child of God, and I am free from every bondage of financial oppression. I ask for divine wisdom to manage my finances and the resources You have entrusted to me. Lord, break the chains of debt in my life and release supernatural provision. Amen.

Scripture: *"The rich rule over the poor, and the borrower is slave to the lender."* (Proverbs 22:7)

"The Spirit you received does not make you slaves, so that you live in fear again; rather, the Spirit you received brought about your adoption to sonship." (Romans 8:15)

6. Prayer Against Generational Locusts

Prayer: Father, I stand in the gap for my family and break every generational curse of loss and destruction caused by locust spirits. I declare that what has been consuming our blessings is broken in the name of Jesus. I ask that You cleanse our bloodline from every locust that has come to destroy our inheritance and prosperity. I speak healing and restoration over my family today, and I claim the freedom to walk in the abundance of Your promises! Amen.

Scripture: *"If you refuse to let my people go, tomorrow I will bring locusts into your country. They shall cover the face of the land, so that no one can see the land."* (Exodus 10:4-5)

7.Prayer for Empowerment and Authority Over Locust Spirits

Prayer: Heavenly Father, I thank You for the authority You have given me over all the powers of the enemy. I declare that I have the power to tread upon every locust spirit that has come to destroy my blessings. I command these spirits to leave my life, my family, and my finances. I receive empowerment from the Holy Spirit to walk in authority and victory. I declare that no locust shall remain in my life, in Jesus' name! Amen.

Scripture: *"Behold, I have given you authority to tread on serpents and scorpions, and over all the power of the enemy, and nothing shall hurt you."* (Luke 10:19)

8. Prayer for Divine Protection

Prayer: Lord, I thank You for Your protection over my life. I declare that I dwell in Your secret place, and I am safe under Your shadow. Protect me from every locust spirit that seeks to invade my life. Keep me hidden from destruction and provide a fortress around my blessings. I trust in Your faithfulness to guard and keep me safe. In Jesus' name, I pray. Amen.

Scripture: *"He who dwells in the secret place of the Most High shall abide under the shadow of the Almighty."* (Psalm 91:1-2)

Scriptures Proving Lack and Poverty Can Be Spiritual and Generational

1. Generational Poverty:
"I, the Lord your God, am a jealous God, punishing the children for the sin of the parents to the third and fourth generation." (Exodus 20:5)

- This shows that generational curses can affect families across generations, and that includes poverty.

2. Poverty as a Spiritual Condition:
"The wealth of the rich is their fortified city, but poverty is the ruin of the poor." (Proverbs 10:15)

- Poverty can be a ruinous spiritual force that destroys lives and futures.

3. Spirit of Poverty:

"Therefore in hunger and thirst, in nakedness and dire poverty, you will serve the enemies the Lord sends against you." (Deuteronomy 28:48)

- This scripture shows that poverty can be a sign of spiritual bondage and oppression.

4. Inherited Poverty Due to Sin:
"In those days people will no longer say, 'The parents have eaten sour grapes, and the children's teeth are set on edge.' Instead, everyone will die for their own sin." (Jeremiah 31:29-30)

- This suggests that generational patterns of sin, including the consequences like poverty, can be broken through repentance and divine intervention.

Day 5: Breaking Baal and Asherah

Ancestral altars in the Bible refer to places or spiritual sites where sacrifices, offerings, or worship were made by ancestors, often associated with their beliefs and practices. These altars are significant in understanding the spiritual legacy that can affect future generations

1. Prayer to Break Ancestral Altars

Prayer: Heavenly Father, I stand in the name of Jesus Christ and break every ancestral altar raised against me and my family. Let every altar speaking evil against my destiny be destroyed by Your power.
Scripture: *"No weapon formed against you shall prosper, and every tongue which rises against you in judgment You shall condemn."* (Isaiah 54:17)

2. Prayer for Deliverance from Generational Curses

Prayer: Lord, I declare that every generational curse connected to ancestral altars is broken in Jesus' name. I cancel every evil covenant and command them to lose their hold over me and my family.
Scripture: *"Christ redeemed us from the curse of the law by becoming a curse for us."* (Galatians 3:13)

3. Prayer to Cancel Evil Sacrifices

Prayer: Father, by the blood of Jesus, I cancel every evil sacrifice made on demonic altars against me or my family. I declare that these sacrifices have no power over me.
Scripture: *"And they overcame him by the blood of the Lamb and by the word of their testimony."* (Revelation 12:11)

4. Prayer to Release Fire on Demonic Altars

Prayer: Lord, send Your consuming fire to destroy every evil altar erected against my life and family. Let every stronghold of darkness be consumed by Your fire.

Scripture: *"For our God is a consuming fire."* (Hebrews 12:29)

5. Prayer for Freedom from Spiritual Bondage

Prayer: In the name of Jesus, I declare freedom from every spiritual bondage connected to evil altars. I claim my liberty and walk in the freedom of the Holy Spirit.

Scripture: *"It is for freedom that Christ has set us free. Stand firm, then, and do not let yourselves be burdened again by a yoke of slavery."* (Galatians 5:1)

6. Prayer to Nullify Covenants with Evil Altars

Prayer: Father, I nullify every covenant made with evil altars, knowingly or unknowingly. I renounce every agreement with the enemy and declare that my life belongs to You.

Scripture: *"Having canceled the charge of our legal indebtedness, which stood against us and condemned us; He has taken it away, nailing it to the cross."* (Colossians 2:14)

7. Prayer to Break Bloodline Ties

Prayer: Lord, I break every bloodline tie that connects me to evil altars from my ancestors. I sever every spiritual link and declare that I am a new creation in Christ.

8. Prayer for Restoration After Breaking Altars

Prayer: Father, after breaking every evil altar, I ask that You restore all that was stolen from me by the enemy. Let blessings flow into my life in abundance.
Scripture: *"I will restore to you the years that the swarming locust has eaten."* (Joel 2:25)

9. Prayer for God's Divine Protection

Prayer: Lord, I declare Your divine protection over me and my family. No evil altar or spirit will have any influence over our lives, for we are covered by Your blood.
Scripture: *"The Lord will keep you from all harm—He will watch over your life."* (Psalm 121:7)

10. Prayer for Establishing God's Altar in My Life

Prayer: Father, I ask that You establish Your divine altar in my life. Let it be an altar of righteousness, holiness, and worship, where Your name is glorified.
Scripture: *"Then build an altar to the Lord your God on the top of this stronghold in an orderly manner."* (Judges 6:26)

11. Prayer for Divine Breakthrough

Prayer: Lord, as I renounce and destroy every evil altar, I pray for breakthrough in every area of my life. Let the chains of limitation be broken, and let Your favor open doors for me.
Scripture: *"The Lord will open the heavens, the storehouse of His bounty, to send rain on your land in season and to bless all the work of your hands."* (Deuteronomy 28:12)

12. Prayer for Victory Over the Enemy

Prayer: In the name of Jesus, I declare victory over every enemy that has risen against me through evil altars. I stand in the authority of Christ and command all demonic forces to flee.

Scripture: *"Behold, I give you the authority to trample on serpents and scorpions, and over all the power of the enemy, and nothing shall by any means hurt you."* (Luke 10:19)

Day 6: Centurion Faith

The Gift Of Faith

The gift of faith is a powerful manifestation of the Holy Spirit that allows believers to trust God beyond natural circumstances. It is a supernatural confidence and assurance that God will act, even in impossible situations. When engaging in spiritual warfare, the gift of faith equips you to stand firm, declare God's promises, and see breakthroughs against all odds.

1. Declaration of God's Power Over Every Battle

Prayer: Father, in the name of Jesus, I declare that You are my ultimate source of strength and victory in every battle. I believe in Your power, and I stand in faith, knowing that You will reward me as I diligently seek You in this spiritual war.
Scripture: *"And without faith it is impossible to please God, because anyone who comes to him must believe that he exists and that he rewards those who earnestly seek him."* (Hebrews 11:6)

2. Binding Every Spirit of Fear

Prayer: By the authority of Jesus Christ, I bind and cast out every spirit of fear and doubt trying to hinder my faith. I declare that fear has no place in my life, for the Lord has given me power, love, and a sound mind.
Scripture: *"For God has not given us a spirit of fear, but of power, love, and a sound mind."* (2 Timothy 1:7)

3. Standing on God's Promises

Prayer: Lord, I stand firm on Your promises today. I declare that every word You have spoken over my life will come to pass. Strengthen my faith to believe and receive Your promises without wavering, increase my faith to see Your wonders.
Scripture: *"For no matter how many promises God has made, they are 'Yes' in Christ."* (2 Corinthians 1:20)

4. Shielding My Mind from Doubt

Prayer: I take up the shield of faith and extinguish every fiery dart of doubt, confusion, and fear sent by the enemy. Lord, cover my mind with the assurance that You are working all things for my good.
Scripture: *"In addition to all this, take up the shield of faith, with which you can extinguish all the flaming arrows of the evil one."* (Ephesians 6:16)

5. Strength to Endure Through Trials

Prayer: Father, I thank You that my faith is being tested and strengthened through every trial. Grant me the endurance to stand firm in the midst of the battle, knowing that my perseverance will bring victory in due time.
Scripture: *"Because you know that the testing of your faith produces perseverance."* (James 1:3)

6. Faith to Overcome Every Circumstance

Prayer: In the name of Jesus, I declare that my faith gives me victory over every circumstance in my life. I am an overcomer through Christ, and nothing can defeat me because my faith is anchored in God.
Scripture: *"For everyone born of God overcomes the world. This is the victory that has overcome the world, even our faith."* (1 John 5:4)

7. Boldness to Speak in Faith

Prayer: Father, I declare that I will speak words of faith and life into every situation. I believe in Your power, and by faith, I decree victory, healing, and breakthrough over my life and the lives of those around me.
Scripture: *"It is written: 'I believed; therefore I have spoken.' Since we have that same spirit of faith, we also believe and therefore speak."* (2 Corinthians 4:13)

8. Activating Faith for Miracles

Prayer: Lord, I activate my faith for the miraculous. I declare that by Your power, miracles will manifest in my life. No situation is too difficult for You, and I stand in faith, expecting to see the impossible become possible.
Scripture: *"If you have faith as small as a mustard seed, you can say to this mountain, 'Move from here to there,' and it will move. Nothing will be impossible for you."* (Matthew 17:20)

9. Declaring Victory Over Spiritual Warfare

Prayer: Father, I stand firm in faith against all the attacks of the enemy. I resist the devil, knowing that I am not alone in this fight. Empower me with unwavering faith as I declare victory in every spiritual battle.
Scripture: *"Resist him, standing firm in the faith, because you know that the family of believers throughout the world is undergoing the same kind of sufferings."* (1 Peter 5:9)

10. Receiving Divine Direction by Faith

Prayer: Lord, by faith, I trust You to guide and direct my steps. Even when I cannot see the way forward, I believe that You are leading me into victory. I submit my plans to You and trust in Your divine wisdom.
Scripture: *"Trust in the Lord with all your heart and lean not on your own understanding; in all your ways submit to him, and he will make your paths straight."* (Proverbs 3:5-6)

11. Faith for Divine Healing

Prayer: In the name of Jesus, I release the prayer of faith for divine healing over my body, my family, and those around me. I declare that sickness and infirmity have no place in my life, and by faith, I receive healing right now.
Scripture: *"And the prayer of faith will save the sick, and the Lord will raise him up."* (James 5:15)

12. Faith to Access the Supernatural

Prayer: Father, I believe that through faith, I have access to the supernatural realm. Let Your power flow through me to perform miracles, signs, and wonders in Your name. Increase my faith to do even greater works than Jesus did on earth.
Scripture: *"Very truly I tell you, whoever believes in me will do the works I have been doing, and they will do even greater things than these, because I am going to the Father."* (John 14:12)

13. Faith for Complete Breakthrough

Prayer: Lord, I declare that by faith, I will see complete breakthrough in every area of my life. Though I may not yet see it, I stand on the evidence of my faith, believing that You are bringing every promise to fulfillment. Nothing is impossible for You, and my breakthrough is on the way.
Scripture: *"Now faith is the substance of things hoped for, the evidence of things not seen."* (Hebrews 11:1)

Day 7: Jospeh Rod

Joseph's journey from being sold into slavery to becoming the second most powerful man in Egypt is a powerful example of arising to influence and impact.

Prayers to Arise in Influence and Impact:

1. Lord, help me to rise in influence so that I may reflect Your light to the world. May my life inspire others to seek You.
"You are the light of the world. A city set on a hill cannot be hidden."
(Matthew 5:14)

2. Father, I pray that my actions and words glorify You, bringing others to recognize Your goodness in my life.
"Let your light shine before others, that they may see your good deeds and glorify your Father in heaven." (Matthew 5:16)

3. Heavenly Father, establish the work of my hands and bless my efforts so that I can positively impact those around me.
"May the favor of the Lord our God rest on us; establish the work of our hands for us—yes, establish the work of our hands." (Psalm 90:17)

4. Lord, I ask for boldness to rise above fear and limitations as I influence others for good, trusting in Your power and strength.
"For God has not given us a spirit of fear, but of power and of love and of a sound mind." (2 Timothy 1:7)

5. Father, as You elevate me, keep me humble and grounded, knowing that all influence and favor come from You.
"Humble yourselves before the Lord, and He will lift you up." (James 4:10)

6. Lord, guide my steps and establish my plans as I seek to make an impact for Your kingdom.
"Commit to the Lord whatever you do, and He will establish your plans."
(Proverbs 16:3)

7. Help me, Father, to serve others with a heart of humility, using my influence to advance Your kingdom and bless those in need.
"The greatest among you will be your servant." (Matthew 23:11)

8. Prayer for Divine Purpose and Vision

Prayer: Father, I thank You for the divine purpose and vision You have for my life. Just as You revealed Joseph's destiny through dreams, reveal Your plans for me and give me the strength to hold on to Your promises, even in difficult times. Let my dreams and purpose be protected by Your power in Jesus' name.
Scripture: *Joseph received dreams from God revealing his future prominence, which gave him the vision and purpose for his life.* (Genesis 37:5-7)
"For I know the plans I have for you, declares the Lord, plans for welfare and not for evil, to give you a future and a hope." (Jeremiah 29:11)

9. Prayer for Endurance in Times of Trials

Prayer: Father, give me the strength and endurance to remain faithful to You in every trial and adversity. Just as Joseph trusted You in the pit and in the prison, help me to trust Your timing and purposes in my life. I rebuke discouragement, despair, and every attempt of the enemy to derail me during difficult seasons. I declare that I will rise from every trial in victory, in Jesus' name.
Scripture: *Count it all joy, my brothers, when you meet trials of various kinds, for you know that the testing of your faith produces steadfastness.* (James 1:2-4)
Scripture Reference: Joseph was thrown into prison unjustly, but he was faithful to God despite the trials he faced. (Genesis 39:20)

10. Prayer for Divine Favor and Influence

Prayer: "Lord, I ask for divine favor in every area of my life. Just as You gave Joseph favor in Potiphar's house, in prison, and in Pharaoh's court, grant me favor before those in authority, in my workplace, and in every place You have called me. Let my life reflect Your favor and glory, and open doors of influence that no man can shut, in Jesus' name."

Scripture: *"But the Lord was with Joseph and showed him steadfast love and gave him favor in the sight of the keeper of the prison."* (Genesis 39:21)

"For you bless the righteous, O Lord; you cover him with favor as with a shield." (Psalm 5:12)

Day 8: Out of the Ashes

Prayer to Rise from Failure

Obed-Edom was a Gittite, and his family rose to prominence after an unexpected blessing from God. In 2 Samuel 6, when King David attempted to bring the Ark of the Covenant to Jerusalem, a man named Uzzah was struck dead for touching the Ark.

1. Heavenly Father, I come to You acknowledging my failures. Help me to learn from my mistakes and rise stronger than before.
Scripture: *"For though the righteous fall seven times, they rise again."* (Proverbs 24:16)

2. Lord, I ask for Your forgiveness for the times I have fallen short. Cleanse my heart and renew my spirit.
Scripture: *"If we confess our sins, He is faithful and just and will forgive us our sins and purify us from all unrighteousness."* (1 John 1:9)

3. Father, grant me the courage to face my failures and the wisdom to understand the lessons they bring.
Scripture: *"And we know that in all things God works for the good of those who love Him, who have been called according to His purpose."* (Romans 8:28)

4. Lord, help me to rise above discouragement and despair. Fill me with hope and a renewed sense of purpose

5. Lord, grant me the grace for a renewal of strength.
Scripture: *"But those who hope in the Lord will renew their strength. They will soar on wings like eagles."* (Isaiah 40:31)

6. Father, I pray for resilience to keep pressing forward, no matter how many times I stumble. Strengthen my faith in You.
Scripture: *"I can do all things through Christ who strengthens me."* (Philippians 4:13)

7. Lord, remind me that my failures do not define me. Help me to see myself through Your eyes, as a beloved child with a purpose.
Scripture: *"For we are God's handiwork, created in Christ Jesus to do good works, which God prepared in advance for us to do."* (Ephesians 2:10)

8. Father, as I rise from failure, may I encourage others who are struggling. Let my testimony be a source of hope and inspiration.
Scripture: *"Praise be to the God and Father of our Lord Jesus Christ, the Father of compassion and the God of all comfort."* (2 Corinthians 1:3)

9. Lord, I thank You for Your grace that allows me to rise again. Help me to trust in Your plan for my life as I move forward.
Scripture: *"The Lord will guide you always; He will satisfy your needs in a sun-scorched land and will strengthen your frame."* (Isaiah 58:11)

Day 9: El Chadash

El Chadash translates to the "God of New" or God of Newness in Hebrew. God is the ultimate creator, bringing order and life from chaos. The act of creation itself is a declaration of new beginnings, setting the foundation for all that follows

Prayer for a New Beginning

1. Heavenly Father, I come to You acknowledging my failures. Help me to learn from my mistakes and rise stronger than before.
Scripture: *" For though the righteous fall seven times, they rise again."* (Proverbs 24:16)

2. Lord, I ask for Your forgiveness for the times I have fallen short. Cleanse my heart and renew my spirit.
Scripture: *"If we confess our sins, He is faithful and just and will forgive us our sins and purify us from all unrighteousness."* (1 John 1:9)

3. Father, grant me the courage to face my failures and the wisdom to understand the lessons they bring.
Scripture: *"And we know that in all things God works for the good of those who love Him, who have been called according to His purpose."* (Romans 8:28)

4. Lord, help me to rise above discouragement and despair. Fill me with hope and a renewed sense of purpose.
Scripture: *"But those who hope in the Lord will renew their strength. They will soar on wings like eagles."* (Isaiah 40:31)

5. Father, I pray for resilience to keep pressing forward, no matter how many times I stumble. Strengthen my faith in You.
Scripture: *"I can do all things through Christ who strengthens me."* (Philippians 4:13)

6. Lord, remind me that my failures do not define me. Help me to see myself through Your eyes, as a beloved child with a purpose.
Scripture: *"For we are God's handiwork, created in Christ Jesus to do good works, which God prepared in advance for us to do."* (Ephesians 2:10)

7.Father, as I rise from failure, may I encourage others who are struggling. Let my testimony be a source of hope and inspiration.
Scripture: *"Praise be to the God and Father of our Lord Jesus Christ, the Father of compassion and the God of all comfort."* (2 Corinthians 1:3)

8.Lord, I thank You for Your grace that allows me to rise again. Help me to trust in Your plan for my life as I move forward.
Scripture: *"The Lord will guide you always; He will satisfy your needs in a sun-scorched land and will strengthen your frame."* (Isaiah 58:11)

9.Prayer for Divine Revelation and Insight

Prayer: Heavenly Father, I come before You seeking divine revelation and insight. Open my eyes to see any hidden obstacles that are fighting my new beginnings. Grant me the wisdom to discern the schemes of the enemy that seek to hinder my progress. I declare that I am equipped with the Spirit of wisdom and revelation, and I will walk in the light of Your truth. In Jesus' name, Amen.
Scripture: *"I keep asking that the God of our Lord Jesus Christ, the glorious Father, may give you the Spirit of wisdom and revelation, so that you may know him better."* (Ephesians 1:17-18)

Day 10: Sidon Hinderance

Sidon had an absence of destiny helpers. Sidon's environment might have stifled any potential for divine intervention or support. This is a hinderance. Destiny helpers are needed.

Prayer for destiny helpers and destiny killers:

1. Father, in every area of my life that I am the one killing my destiny, let my eyes be opened today and give me grace to make amends in the name of Jesus.

2. Father, every destiny killer from my root around my life, if they refuse to repent, send them on the journey of no return in the name of Jesus.

3. Father, the helper of my destiny, before the end of this week, that man, you have ordained to help me from the beginning must locate me by your power in the name of Jesus.

4. Every satanic garment that covered my parent's destiny and is covering my own destiny, you are a liar, be removed and catch fire in the name of Jesus.

5. In the name of Jesus, every rag the enemy has put on my destiny catch fire, my destiny refuse to wear rags in the name of Jesus.

6. Any man or woman, power or spirit, standing between my helper and I, your time is up, be uprooted out of my way in the name of Jesus.

7. Prayer Against Generational Curses

Prayer: In the name of Jesus, I break every generational curse that has hindered my destiny. I declare that I am not bound by the failures of my ancestors, and I step into the fullness of what God has for me!

Scripture: *"Christ has redeemed us from the curse of the law, having become a curse for us."* (Galatians 3:13, NKJV)

8. Prayer for Divine Helpers to Locate You

Prayer: Father, in this season, let divine connections be established. I call forth every helper that You have ordained for me. Before this month ends, let them locate me by Your divine power in the name of Jesus!
Scripture: *"The king's heart is in the hand of the Lord, like the rivers of water; He turns it wherever He wishes."* (Proverbs 21:1, NKJV)

9. Prayer Against Spiritual Attacks on Your Destiny

Prayer: Every spirit of delay and distraction assigned to my destiny, I command you to be dismantled and cast out of my life in the name of Jesus. My purpose shall not be hindered!

10. Prayer Against the Spirit of Confusion

Prayer: I come against every spirit of confusion that clouds the judgment of my destiny helpers. I declare that their minds are clear and focused on helping me as God has ordained in the name of Jesus!
Scripture: *"For God is not the author of confusion but of peace, as in all the churches of the saints."* (1 Corinthians 14:33, NKJV)

11. Prayer Against Manipulation

Prayer: Every spirit of manipulation that seeks to influence my destiny helpers against me, I bind you in the name of Jesus! I declare that they will see the truth and be inclined to assist me!
Scripture: *"And you will know the truth, and the truth will set you free."* (John 8:32, ESV)

12. Prayer for Open Hearts

Prayer: Father, open the hearts of those You have ordained to help me. Let them be willing to assist me in every way possible in the name of Jesus!
Scripture: *"And the Lord gave the people favor in the sight of the Egyptians."* (Exodus 12:36, NKJV)

13. Prayer Against Manipulation

Prayer: Every spirit of manipulation that seeks to influence my destiny helpers against me, I bind you in the name of Jesus! I declare that they will see the truth and be inclined to assist me!
Scripture: *"And you will know the truth, and the truth will set you free."* (John 8:32, ESV)

14. Prayer for Open Hearts

Prayer: Father, open the hearts of those You have ordained to help me. Let them be willing to assist me in every way possible in the name of Jesus!
Scripture: *"And the Lord gave the people favor in the sight of the Egyptians."* (Exodus 12:36, NKJV)

15. Prayer Against Distractions

Prayer: In the name of Jesus, I come against every distraction that is preventing my destiny helpers from focusing on their assignment to assist me. Let their eyes be opened to see their role in my life!
Scripture: *"But one thing is needed, and Mary has chosen that good part, which will not be taken away from her."* (Luke 10:42, NKJV)

16. Prayer for Uprooting Negative Influences

Prayer: Every negative influence that is causing my destiny helpers to hesitate in helping me, I command you to be uprooted and cast out in the name of Jesus!
Scripture: *"Every plant which My heavenly Father has not planted will be uprooted."* (Matthew 15:13, NKJV)
"Arise, shine, for your light has come, and the glory of the Lord rises upon you." (Isaiah 60:1, NIV)

17. Prayer for Uprooting of Destiny Killers

Prayer: Father, every destiny killer in my life, whether known or unknown, I command you to be uprooted by fire and cast out of my life in the name of Jesus!
Scripture: *"Every plant which My heavenly Father has not planted will be uprooted."* (Matthew 15:13, NKJV)

18. Prayer for Restoration of Stolen Opportunities

Prayer: Lord, restore every opportunity that has been stolen from me by the enemy. I reclaim my lost opportunities, and I declare that they will come to me in the name of Jesus!
Scripture: *"I will restore to you the years that the swarming locust has eaten."* (Joel 2:25, ESV)

19. Prayer for Divine Direction

Prayer: Father, guide my steps toward the helpers You have ordained for me. Lead me to the right places and people that will assist in fulfilling my destiny in the name of Jesus!

20. Prayer Against Confusion and Misunderstandings

Prayer: Every spirit of confusion and misunderstanding that is affecting my relationships with my destiny helpers, I bind you and cast you out in the name of Jesus! Let clarity and understanding reign!
Scripture: *"For God is not the author of confusion but of peace."*
(1 Corinthians 14:33, NKJV)

21. Prayer for Favor with Destiny Helpers

Prayer: Father, grant me favor in the sight of those You have chosen to help me. Let them see my value and be inclined to assist me in my endeavors in the name of Jesus!
Scripture: *"And the Lord gave the people favor in the sight of the Egyptians."*
(Exodus 12:36, NKJV)

22. Prayer for Open Hearts

Prayer: Father, open the hearts of those You have ordained to help me. Let them be willing to assist me in every way possible in the name of Jesus!
Scripture: *"And the Lord gave the people favor in the sight of the Egyptians."*
(Exodus 12:36, NKJV)

Day 11: Nehemiah's Strength

God's strength will always assures believers like you and I of victory. Many circumstances where the strength of God was evident. You will be apart of God's track record this year as it pertains to this super natural strength.

Divine Strength

1. Prayer for Strength in Weakness

Prayer: Heavenly Father, I acknowledge my weaknesses and ask for Your divine strength to sustain me. In my moments of weakness, let Your power be made perfect in my life. Empower me to rise above my challenges in the name of Jesus!
Scripture: *"But he said to me, 'My grace is sufficient for you, for my power is made perfect in weakness.'"* (2 Corinthians 12:9, ESV)

2. Prayer for Strength to Endure Trials

Prayer: Lord, grant me the strength to endure trials and tribulations. Help me to remain steadfast and unmovable in faith, trusting that You are with me through every storm in the name of Jesus!
Scripture: *"Blessed is the man who remains steadfast under trial, for when he has stood the test he will receive the crown of life."* (James 1:12, ESV)

3. Prayer for Strength in Serving Others

Prayer: Father, empower me with the strength to serve others selflessly. Let Your love flow through me, enabling me to uplift and support those around me, even when I feel weary in the name of Jesus!
Scripture: *"The steps of a good man are ordered by the Lord."* (Psalm 37:23, NKJV)

Boldness and Courage:

1. Prayer for Boldness in Proclaiming the Gospel

Prayer: Father, in the name of Jesus, grant me the courage to speak Your Word with boldness and clarity. Just as You empowered Peter and John, fill me with the confidence to proclaim Your truth, regardless of opposition or fear. Strengthen me to preach Your gospel without compromise, trusting in Your power to guide and protect me. Amen.

Scripture : *"Now, Lord, consider their threats and enable your servants to speak your word with great boldness."* (Acts 4:29, NIV)

2. Prayer Against the Spirit of Fear

Prayer: Lord, I reject every spirit of fear that seeks to hinder my boldness in Your work. I declare that fear has no place in my heart because You have given me a spirit of power, love, and sound mind. I step out in faith, trusting that You are with me, and I will not be intimidated by any opposition in Jesus' name. Amen.

Scripture : *"For God has not given us a spirit of fear, but of power and of love and of a sound mind."* (2 Timothy 1:7, NKJV)

3. Prayer for Courage in Persecution

Prayer: Father, when persecution arises because of my stand for Your kingdom, give me the strength to endure with joy. Empower me to remain steadfast in faith like the apostles, who faced persecution but did not waver. Let my testimony glorify You, and may I continue to preach Your Word with unwavering boldness in the face of trials. In Jesus' name, Amen.

Scripture : *"Blessed are those who are persecuted because of righteousness, for theirs is the kingdom of heaven."* (Matthew 5:10, NIV)

4. Prayer for Apostolic Strength and Courage in Spiritual Warfare

Prayer: Lord, grant me apostolic courage as I engage in spiritual warfare. Clothe me with Your full armor—truth, righteousness, faith, salvation, and the sword of the Spirit. Strengthen my resolve to stand firm against the enemy's schemes and give me the spiritual discernment to fight victoriously. May Your power be made perfect in me.

Scripture : "*Be strong in the Lord and in his mighty power. Put on the full armor of God, so that you can take your stand against the devil's schemes.*" (Ephesians 6:10-11, NIV)

5. Prayer for Divine Wisdom and Courage

Prayer: Heavenly Father, as You granted wisdom to the apostles, give me wisdom and discernment in all my endeavors. Help me to navigate challenges with the boldness that comes from knowing I am walking in Your will. Let Your wisdom guide my decisions, and may I never shrink back in fear but act with apostolic courage in every situation, for the glory of Your name. Amen.

Scripture : "*If any of you lacks wisdom, let him ask of God, who gives to all liberally and without reproach, and it will be given to him.*" (James 1:5, NKJV)

6. Prayer for Strength to Overcome Opposition

Prayer: Lord, in times of opposition, give me the strength and courage to stand firm in my faith. Even when I am pressed on every side, I will not be crushed, for You are my shield and my defender. Strengthen my inner man, and grant me the resilience of Paul, who overcame adversity with grace and courage. Let my testimony reflect Your strength in my life. Amen.

Scripture : "*We are hard pressed on every side, but not crushed; perplexed, but not in despair; persecuted, but not abandoned; struck down, but not destroyed.*" (2 Corinthians 4:8-9, NIV)

7. Prayer for Courage to Fulfill Divine Purpose

Prayer: Father, as You led the apostles to fulfill their divine assignments, lead me with courage to fulfill my purpose, no matter the cost. Even when I do not know what the future holds, give me the faith to trust in Your plan for my life. Help me walk in obedience, as Paul did, knowing that You are with me through every hardship and trial. Amen.

Scripture : *"And now, compelled by the Spirit, I am going to Jerusalem, not knowing what will happen to me there. I only know that in every city the Holy Spirit warns me that prison and hardships are facing me."* (Acts 20:22-23, NIV)

8. Prayer for Boldness in Prayer and Intercession

Prayer: Father, grant me boldness in prayer and intercession. I approach Your throne with confidence, knowing that You hear my prayers. Give me the strength to stand in the gap for others, praying with apostolic authority and declaring Your will over my life and the lives of those around me. Let my prayers shake the heavens and bring about divine intervention. In Jesus' name, Amen.

Scripture : *"Let us therefore come boldly to the throne of grace, that we may obtain mercy and find grace to help in time of need."* (Hebrews 4:16, NKJV)

9. Prayer for the Power of the Holy Spirit

Prayer: Holy Spirit, fill me with the power and courage that comes from Your presence. As the apostles were empowered to spread the gospel to the ends of the earth, fill me with the same courage and zeal. Let the fire of the Holy Spirit embolden me to witness without fear, and may Your power flow through me as I carry out the great commission. Amen.

Scripture : *"But you will receive power when the Holy Spirit comes on you; and you will be my witnesses in Jerusalem, and in all Judea and Samaria, and to the ends of the earth."* (Acts 1:8, NIV)

10. Prayer for Breakthrough and Courage in Uncertain Times

Prayer: Lord, in times of uncertainty and doubt, strengthen my confidence in You. Give me the courage to persevere through every trial, knowing that You will reward my faithfulness. Help me to stand firm in Your promises, trusting that You are working all things for my good. Let Your courage flow through me as I await the fulfillment of Your promises. Amen.

Scripture: *"So do not throw away your confidence; it will be richly rewarded. You need to persevere so that when you have done the will of God, you will receive what he has promised."* (Hebrews 10:35-36, NIV)

Day 12: Field of Boaz

Change My Story: Lord, I believe in Your power to transform lives and situations. Just as You promised in Isaiah 43:19, I trust that You are doing a new thing in my life.

1. Prayer for Divine Guidance

Prayer: Father, I ask for Your divine guidance in every decision I need to make. Lead me clearly and help me discern Your will in my life. (Proverbs 3:5-6)

2. Prayer for Breakthrough

Prayer: Lord, I declare a breakthrough in every area of my life where I am facing obstacles. Intervene, O God, and make a way where there seems to be no way. (Isaiah 43:16)

3. Prayer for Healing

Prayer: Heavenly Father, I ask for Your divine intervention in my health. Bring healing and restoration to my body and soul, just as You did for the woman with the issue of blood. (Mark 5:34)

4. Prayer for Deliverance from Oppression

Prayer:In the name of Jesus, I break every chain of oppression and bondage in my life. I pray for Your divine intervention to set me free from every form of spiritual captivity. (Isaiah 61:1)

5. Prayer for Restoration

Prayer: Lord, restore what has been lost in my life, whether it be relationships, finances, or dreams. Bring back the years the locusts have eaten. (Joel 2:25)

6. Prayer for Protection

Prayer: Father, I ask for Your divine protection over my life, family, and belongings. Shield us from harm and danger, and let Your angels encamp around us. (Psalm 91:11)

7. Prayer for Wisdom and Understanding

Prayer: O God, grant me wisdom and understanding to navigate through life's challenges. I seek Your divine intervention in making choices that honor You. (James 1:5)

8. Prayer for Financial Breakthrough

Prayer: Lord, I pray for divine intervention in my finances. Open doors of opportunity, provide for my needs, and bless the work of my hands. (Philippians 4:19)

9. Prayer for Family Restoration

Prayer: Heavenly Father, intervene in my family situation. Heal broken relationships, bring unity, and restore love and harmony in our home. (Ephesians 4:3)

10. Prayer for Peace in Troubling Times

Prayer: Jesus, I ask for Your peace that surpasses all understanding to guard my heart and mind. Intervene in the chaos around me and give me Your tranquility. (Philippians 4:6-7)

11. Prayer for Courage and Boldness

Prayer: God, grant me divine courage to face challenges and speak boldly for You. Help me to overcome fear and step out in faith as You direct my path. (Acts 4:29)

12. Prayer for Restoration of Destiny

Prayer: Father, intervene in my destiny and restore every stolen or lost opportunity. Align me with Your divine purpose for my life. (Jeremiah 29:11)

13. Prayer for a Fresh Anointing

Prayer: Lord, anoint me afresh with Your Holy Spirit. Empower me to fulfill Your call on my life and to walk in Your divine favor. (Acts 1:8)

14. Prayer for Spiritual Revival

Prayer: Holy Spirit, revive my spirit and draw me closer to You. Intervene in my life and refresh my passion for You and Your Word. (Psalm 85:6)

15. Prayer for Deliverance from Fear

Prayer: In the name of Jesus, I bind and cast out the spirit of fear from my life. Fill me with Your love and sound mind as You intervene in my fears. (2 Timothy 1:7)

Fiery Furnace
Divine Intervention

1. Prayer for Awareness of God's Presence
Prayer: Father, open my eyes to see the ways You are intervening in my life. Help me to recognize Your presence and guidance in every situation. (Psalm 119:18)

2. Prayer for Divine Help in Crisis
Prayer: O God, I call upon You in my time of trouble. Intervene in this situation and provide the help I need. (Psalm 50:15)

3. Prayer Against Obstacles
Prayer: Every obstacle standing in the way of my breakthrough, I command you to be removed by the power of God. (Mark 11:23)

4. Prayer for Faith to Believe
Prayer: Lord, increase my faith to believe in Your power to intervene. Help me to trust in Your goodness and mercy. (Luke 17:5)

5. Prayer for Protection and Deliverance
Prayer: I declare that I am protected by the blood of Jesus. Every plan of the enemy to hinder my progress is thwarted in Jesus' name. (Psalm 91:3-4)

6. Prayer for Restoration of Lost Opportunities
Prayer: Heavenly Father, I pray for Your divine intervention to restore every lost opportunity in my life. Bring back what the enemy has stolen. (Joel 2:25)

7. Prayer for Guidance in Confusion
Prayer: Lord, I am confused and do not know what to do. I seek Your guidance and ask that You intervene and lead me in the right direction. (Proverbs 3:5-6)

8. Prayer for Divine Deliverance

Prayer: Heavenly Father, just as You delivered Shadrach, Meshach, and Abednego from the flames, I ask for Your divine deliverance in my life. Rescue me from any fiery trials and let Your glory be revealed through my situation.
Scripture: *"The Lord is my rock, my fortress and my deliverer."*
(2 Samuel 22:2, NIV)

Day 13: Potiphar's Wife

Potiphar's wife represents the decoy that can divert individuals from their God-given purpose.

Her advances are not just personal but also test Joseph's character and commitment to God.

Decoys:
1. Prayer for Divine Revelation

Prayer: Heavenly Father, I ask for the spirit of wisdom and revelation. Open my eyes to see every destiny decoy in my life and grant me the insight to avoid their traps. Reveal to me those who are not aligned with Your purpose for me.
Scripture: Ephesians 1:17-18 (Spirit of wisdom and revelation)

2. Prayer for Protection from Deceptive Influences

Prayer: Lord, protect me from every deceptive influence that seeks to derail my destiny. Surround me with Your divine protection, guiding my steps and keeping me safe from harmful intentions.
Scripture: Psalm 121:7-8 (The Lord will protect)

3. Prayer for Discernment

Prayer: Father, fill my heart with love that is accompanied by knowledge and discernment. Help me to identify those who might masquerade as friends but are actually decoys meant to distract me from my purpose.
Scripture: Philippians 1:9-10 (Love with knowledge and discernment)

4. Prayer for Deliverance from Manipulation

Prayer: Lord, deliver me from the snare of the fowler and from every manipulation aimed at my destiny. Break every chain of deception that seeks to keep me from fulfilling Your will in my life.
Scripture: Psalm 91:3 (Deliverance from the snare)

5. Prayer for Clear Direction

Prayer: I trust in You, Lord, with all my heart and lean not on my own understanding. Direct my paths and show me the way to fulfill my destiny, away from every decoy that distracts me from Your purpose.
Scripture: Proverbs 3:5-6 (Trust in the Lord)

6. Prayer for Divine Connections

Prayer: Lord, bring the right people into my life who will support and encourage me in my destiny. Remove every decoy that would lead me to toxic relationships and unproductive connections.
Scripture: Ecclesiastes 4:9-10 (Two are better than one)

Day 14: Balm in Gilead

Supernatural restoration of health that comes from God. Jesus' ministry was marked by acts of healing, showcasing divine healing in action. Divine healing can also extend to emotional and psychological wounds, such as trauma, grief, depression, and anxiety.

1. Healing from Cancer
Prayer: Heavenly Father, I bring before You those battling cancer. I ask for Your healing touch to be upon them. May every cancerous cell be destroyed by Your mighty power. According to Isaiah 53:5, by Your stripes, they are healed.
Scripture: "*But He was pierced for our transgressions, He was crushed for our iniquities; the punishment that brought us peace was on Him, and by His wounds, we are healed.*" (Psalm 147:3)

2. Healing of the Heart

Prayer: Lord, I pray for those struggling with heart issues. May Your healing flow through their cardiovascular system, bringing strength and vitality. Restore their hearts to perfect health.
Scripture: "*He heals the brokenhearted and binds up their wounds.*" (Psalm 147:3)

3. Healing of the Lungs

Prayer: Father, I lift up those suffering from respiratory diseases. Heal their lungs and restore their breath. Let every breath they take be a reminder of Your healing power.
Scripture: "*The Spirit of God has made me; the breath of the Almighty gives me life.*" (Job 33:4)

Men of our Day:

Smith Wigglesworth was a prominent evangelist and faith healer in the early 20th century, known for his powerful healing ministry and his strong emphasis on faith. His life and ministry were marked by many accounts of miraculous healings. Here are some notable stories of healing associated with Smith Wigglesworth:

1. The Healing of a Deaf Mute
One of the most famous accounts involved a man who was deaf and mute. Wigglesworth prayed for him, and after several attempts, he commanded the man to speak and hear in Jesus' name. The man began to hear and speak clearly. This miraculous healing not only transformed the man's life but also encouraged others to believe in the power of prayer and faith.

2. Raising the Dead
Wigglesworth had several accounts of praying for the dead. In one notable incident, he was called to pray for a woman who had been pronounced dead. He arrived to find her family grieving. Wigglesworth prayed fervently and commanded the woman to rise. To everyone's astonishment, she awoke and sat up, restoring life to her body. This event showcased not only the power of faith but also the belief in God's sovereignty over life and death. And depth of Wigglesworth's faith and his belief in divine healing.

3. Healing a Woman with a Tumor
A woman with a large tumor sought Wigglesworth's help. He prayed for her and instructed her to believe in her healing. The tumor was visible and painful, but after several prayers and declarations of faith, the woman reported that she felt a warmth in her body. When she returned a few days later, the tumor had completely disappeared, confirming her healing.

4. The Blind Woman
Wigglesworth encountered a woman who was completely blind. He prayed for her, but she did not immediately regain her sight. Undeterred, he prayed multiple times and urged her to have faith. Eventually, her sight was restored, and she could see clearly. This story illustrates Wigglesworth's tenacity in prayer and his belief that faith could lead to miraculous outcomes.

5. Healing the Paralytic
In another account, Wigglesworth prayed for a man who was paralyzed and unable to walk. After praying for him, Wigglesworth commanded him to stand and walk in faith. Initially hesitant, the man eventually rose and took a few steps, to the amazement of everyone present. His faith, combined with Wigglesworth's confident prayers, resulted in a powerful healing.

6. Multiple Healings in One Meeting
During a revival meeting, Wigglesworth witnessed numerous healings in one service. He called people to come forward for prayer, and one by one, individuals with various ailments, including arthritis, blindness, and cancer, reported being healed. The atmosphere was charged with faith, and many were transformed both physically and spiritually.

7. The Healing of His Own Wife
Smith Wigglesworth's wife, Polly, was also a key figure in his life. After she passed away, he reportedly raised her from the dead shortly after her death, demonstrating his unwavering faith. Although she returned to life briefly, she told him to let her go, indicating she wanted to be with the Lord. This personal story illustrates the profound.

Day 15: Sons of Belial

By aligning your words with God's truth and authority, you can declare victory over wickedness and assert your identity as a child of God. The influence of Belial shall not pass to my children or grandchildren.

1. Prayer for Truth to Prevail:

Prayer: Heavenly Father, I ask that Your truth be revealed in every situation where lies and deception have been spoken against me. Let Your light expose the darkness of deceit.

Scripture: *"Then you will know the truth, and the truth will set you free."* (John 8:32)

2. Prayer for Protection Against Slander:

Prayer: Lord, protect me from the schemes of the sons of Belial. Guard my heart and mind against lies and slander that may arise from others.

Scripture: *"Keep me, O Lord, from the hands of the wicked; preserve me from violent men who have planned to trip up my feet."* (Psalm 140:4)

3. Prayer for Discernment:

Prayer: Father, grant me discernment to recognize the lies of the enemy and the tactics of seducing spirits. Help me to see through falsehoods and stand firm in Your truth.

Scripture: *"Dear friends, do not believe every spirit, but test the spirits to see whether they are from God..."* (1 John 4:1)

4. Prayer for Restoration of Reputation

Prayer: Lord, I pray for the restoration of my reputation where it has been tarnished by lies. Bring forth truth and vindicate me in the eyes of those who matter.

Scripture: *"He will make your righteous reward shine like the dawn, your vindication like the noonday sun."* (Psalm 37:6)

74

5. Prayer for Strength Against Doubt:

Prayer: God, strengthen my faith and confidence in who I am in You. Help me to reject any lies that undermine my identity as Your beloved child.
Scripture: *"For God has not given us a spirit of fear, but of power and of love and of a sound mind."* (2 Timothy 1:7)

6. Prayer for the Exposure of Lies

Prayer: Lord, I ask that You expose every lie spoken against me by the sons of Belial. Let Your truth shine through the darkness and reveal the deceitful tactics of the enemy.
Scripture: *"But everything exposed by the light becomes visible—and everything that is illuminated becomes a light."* (Ephesians 5:13)

7. Prayer for Deliverance from Manipulation

Prayer: Father, deliver me from the manipulation and influence of the sons of Belial. Break every chain of bondage that they may have tried to place on my life and set me free by Your power.
Scripture: *"Is not this the kind of fasting I have chosen: to loose the chains of injustice and untie the cords of the yoke, to set the oppressed free and break every yoke?"* (Isaiah 58:6)

Prayer Points Against the Sons of Belial in Your Marriage:

1. Prayer for Protection of the Marriage

Prayer: Heavenly Father, I ask for Your divine protection over my marriage. Shield us from the influence of the sons of Belial that seek to sow discord and confusion between us.
Scripture: *"Unless the Lord builds the house, the builders labor in vain."*
(Psalm 127:1)

2. Prayer for Unity and Agreement

Prayer: Lord, I pray for unity in our marriage. Remove any influences that seek to divide us, and help us to stand in agreement with one another as we seek Your will together.
Scripture: *"Do two walk together unless they have agreed to do so?"* (Amos 3:3)

3. Prayer for Exposure of Deceit

Prayer: Father, expose any lies or deceit that the sons of Belial may be trying to use against our marriage. Let the truth shine forth, and help us to recognize any manipulative tactics at work.
Scripture: *"And you will know the truth, and the truth will set you free."*
(John 8:32)

4. Prayer for Restoration and Healing

Prayer: Lord, I ask for restoration in our marriage where there has been hurt or misunderstanding. Heal any wounds caused by lies or manipulation, and help us to rebuild our relationship on a foundation of love and trust.
Scripture: *"But I will restore you to health and heal your wounds,' declares the Lord..."* (Jeremiah 30:17)

5. Prayer for Divine Wisdom

Prayer: God, grant us wisdom to navigate the challenges we face in our marriage. Help us to discern the voice of the enemy from Your voice, and guide us in making decisions that honor You and each other.
Scripture: "*If any of you lacks wisdom, you should ask God, who gives generously to all without finding fault, and it will be given to you.*" (James 1:5)

6. Prayer Against Division and Strife

Prayer: In the name of Jesus, I bind and rebuke any spirit of division or strife that the sons of Belial may be trying to introduce into our marriage. Let peace reign in our home.
Scripture: "*Make every effort to keep the unity of the Spirit through the bond of peace.*" (Ephesians 4:3)

7. Prayer for Godly Counsel

Prayer: Lord, surround us with wise and godly counsel that will support and strengthen our marriage. Remove any negative influences that would lead us astray or cause us to doubt each other.
Scripture: "*Plans fail for lack of counsel, but with many advisers, they succeed.*" (Proverbs 15:22)

8. Prayer for a Strong Spiritual Foundation

Prayer: Heavenly Father, strengthen our spiritual foundation as a couple. Help us to seek You together in prayer and study, so that no evil influence can separate us.
Scripture: "*Therefore everyone who hears these words of mine and puts them into practice is like a wise man who built his house on the rock.*" (Matthew 7:24)

Day 15: Warfare Prayers Against Discouragement:

1. Prayer for Divine Intervention

Prayer: In the mighty name of Jesus, I command every spirit of discouragement to be uprooted from my life. I declare that the fire of the Holy Spirit burns away every negative thought and feeling that the enemy has planted in my mind. Let divine intervention occur NOW! Every dark cloud of despair, be scattered by the thunder of God's power!
Scripture: "*No weapon forged against you will prevail, and you will refute every tongue that accuses you.*" (Isaiah 54:17)

2. Prayer to Break Strongholds

Prayer: I pull down every stronghold of discouragement in my life, in the name of Jesus! I break the chains of negativity and defeat that the enemy has placed upon me. Fire of God, consume every spirit of heaviness that tries to keep me down. I arise in the power of the Holy Ghost!
Scripture: "*The weapons we fight with are not the weapons of the world. On the contrary, they have divine power to demolish strongholds.*" (2 Corinthians 10:4)

3. Prayer for Restoration of Joy

Prayer: Heavenly Father, restore my joy! I command every demon of discouragement to flee from my life! In the name of Jesus, I declare that joy floods my soul, and the oil of gladness replaces every spirit of heaviness. Let the fire of revival ignite within me!
Scripture: "*You turned my wailing into dancing; you removed my sackcloth and cloth me with joy.*" (Psalm 30:11)

4. Prayer for Divine Protection

Prayer: Lord, I declare that I am hidden under Your wings. I bind every spirit of discouragement that has come to attack my mind and heart. In the name of Jesus, I declare that no weapon formed against me shall prosper. Let the thunder of God arise against every attack of the enemy!
Scripture: "*Whoever dwells in the secret place of the Most High will rest in the shadow of the Almighty.*" (Psalm 91:1-3)

5. Prayer for Fire to Consume the Enemy

Prayer: I call down the fire of God to consume every demonic orchestrator of discouragement! I command every plan of the enemy to be dismantled and destroyed. Let the consuming fire of the Holy Ghost burn every barrier to my peace and joy!
Scripture: "*For our God is a consuming fire.*" (Hebrews 12:29)

6. Prayer for Empowerment and Strength

Prayer: I declare that I am empowered by the Holy Spirit to rise above discouragement! Every spirit of defeat, I command you to leave now! I am more than a conqueror through Christ who strengthens me. Let the fire of God rise within me and strengthen my resolve!
Scripture: "*No, in all these things we are more than conquerors through him who loved us.*" (Romans 8:37)

7. Prayer for a New Season

Prayer: I declare a new season of hope and encouragement in my life! Every demonic influence that seeks to keep me in a state of discouragement, I bind you and cast you out! In the name of Jesus, I step into the light of God's favor and grace!
Scripture: "*Forget the former things; do not dwell on the past. See, I am doing a new thing!*" (Isaiah 43:18-19)

8. Prayer for Divine Strategies

Prayer: Lord, give me divine strategies to overcome every discouragement. I call forth the wisdom and guidance of the Holy Spirit to lead me out of this valley of despair. In the name of Jesus, let the plans of the enemy be thwarted and turned to dust!
Scripture: "*Trust in the Lord with all your heart and lean not on your own understanding; in all your ways submit to him, and he will make your paths straight.*" (Proverbs 3:5-6)

9. Prayer for Restoration and Healing

Prayer: Lord, I ask for restoration in our marriage where there has been hurt or misunderstanding. Heal any wounds caused by lies or manipulation, and help us to rebuild our relationship on a foundation of love and trust.
Scripture: "*But I will restore you to health and heal your wounds,' declares the Lord...*" (Jeremiah 30:17)

10. Prayer for Divine Wisdom

Prayer: God, grant us wisdom to navigate the challenges we face in our marriage. Help us to discern the voice of the enemy from Your voice, and guide us in making decisions that honor You and each other.
Scripture: "If any of you lacks wisdom, you should ask God, who gives generously to all without finding fault, and it will be given to you." (James 1:5)

11. Prayer Against Division and Strife

Prayer: In the name of Jesus, I bind and rebuke any spirit of division or strife that the sons of Belial may be trying to introduce into our marriage. Let peace reign in our home.
Scripture: "*Make every effort to keep the unity of the Spirit through the bond of peace.*" (Ephesians 4:3)

Day 16: Josiah Generation

Josiah became king of Judah at a young age and was noted for his righteousness. He initiated significant reforms, including restoring the worship of Yahweh and removing idols from the temple. His heart was inclined toward God from early on, and he led the nation back to proper worship.

1. Prayer for Salvation

Prayer: Father, in the mighty name of Jesus, I declare that my children shall be saved! I command every stronghold of darkness holding their souls captive to be shattered by fire and thunder! Let the light of the Gospel penetrate their hearts, leading them to salvation. Every plan of the enemy to divert them from Your path, be destroyed now in Jesus' name!

2. Prayer for Health

Prayer: O Lord, I invoke the fire of God to consume every sickness and disease that seeks to afflict my children! By the stripes of Jesus, they are healed! I declare divine health over their bodies, minds, and spirits. Every curse of infirmity be broken by the thunder of heaven! Let every organ function perfectly as designed by You in Jesus' name!

3. Prayer for Education

Prayer: In the name of Jesus, I decree that my children shall excel in their studies! I send forth fire to consume every spirit of confusion and distraction that hinders their learning. Let the wisdom of God fill their minds and hearts. Thunder, arise and strike every negative influence affecting their education! I declare that they will be at the top of their class, in Jesus' name!

4. Prayer for Good Friends

Prayer: Lord, I pray for divine connections for my children. Bring them good friends who will uplift and encourage them in their faith. I strike down every plan of the enemy to lead them into bad company. Fire and thunder, arise and scatter any negative influences around them! Let their friendships be rooted in Your love and guidance, in the name of Jesus!

5. Prayer Against Bad Friends

Prayer: Every evil friend and negative influence sent to mislead my children, I command you to be uprooted by the fire of God! Thunder, strike every relationship that does not align with Your will for their lives! I declare that my children will discern good from evil and choose friends who will lead them to righteousness and success in Jesus' name!

6. Prayer for Future Spouses

Prayer: Heavenly Father, I cover my children's future spouses in prayer! I declare that they will be godly partners, rooted in Your love and wisdom. By fire, I cleanse their paths from any negative influences or distractions that would lead them away from the spouse You have chosen for them. Thunder of heaven, strike every deception that would hinder their divine connection in the name of Jesus!

7. Prayer for Protection

Prayer: I decree divine protection over my children in every area of their lives! Surround them with Your angels, Lord. I command every plan of the enemy against their safety to be thwarted by fire and thunder! No weapon formed against them shall prosper! Let them dwell in the secret place of the Most High, under Your shadow, in Jesus' name!

8. Prayer for Wisdom and Discernment

Prayer: Lord, grant my children wisdom beyond their years. I call forth the fire of the Holy Spirit to ignite a spirit of discernment in their hearts. Every lie of the enemy that seeks to cloud their judgment, I strike it down with the thunder of God! Let them always choose Your ways and walk in Your truth, in Jesus' name!

9. Prayer for Protection from Bad Influences

Prayer: Heavenly Father, I come before You, asking for divine protection from all bad influences in my life and the lives of my loved ones. In the name of Jesus, I declare that every negative voice, every harmful relationship, and every corrupting influence is broken by the fire of the Holy Spirit! Let Your thunder strike every plan of the enemy to entangle us in darkness. I plead the blood of Jesus over our minds, hearts, and paths. We shall walk in Your light and truth!

Scripture: *"He who walks with wise men will be wise, but the companion of fools will be destroyed".* (Proverbs 13:20)

10. Prayer Against Peer Pressure

Prayer: In the mighty name of Jesus, I come against every spirit of peer pressure that seeks to manipulate or control my decisions and actions. I strike down every influence that contradicts Your will for my life. Fire, arise and consume every urge to conform to the world! Thunder, break every chain that binds me to unhealthy expectations. I declare my freedom and commitment to follow Christ above all!

Scripture: *"For do I now persuade men, or God? Or do I seek to please men? For if I still pleased men, I would not be a bondservant of Christ"* (Galatians 1:10)

11. Prayer for Deliverance from Toxic Relationships

Prayer: Father, I ask for deliverance from every toxic relationship that is dragging me away from You. In the name of Jesus, I sever every ungodly connection with the fire of God! Thunder, strike every relationship that does not bring glory to Your name. I declare that I will surround myself with godly influences, and I release myself from any bond with those who do not walk in Your light.

Scripture: *"Do not be unequally yoked together with unbelievers. For what fellowship has righteousness with lawlessness? And what communion has light with darkness?"* (2 Corinthians 6:14)

12. Prayer for Strength to Resist Negative Influences

Prayer: Lord, I ask for Your strength to resist every negative influence that seeks to pull me away from Your purpose. I clothe myself in Your armor, and with fire, I strike down every temptation and negative influence. Thunder of heaven, empower me to stand firm and not yield to the pressures of the enemy! I declare that I am strong in the Lord and in the power of His might!

Scripture: *"Finally, my brethren, be strong in the Lord and in the power of His might. Put on the whole armor of God, that you may be able to stand against the wiles of the devil".* (Ephesians 6:10-11)

13. Prayer for Restoration and Healing

Prayer: Gracious Father, I pray for restoration and healing from the wounds caused by bad influences in my life. Let Your fire cleanse my heart and mind from the damage done. Thunder of God, echo through my soul, bringing forth healing and renewal. I declare that I am whole and restored, and I will no longer be influenced by darkness but will walk in Your light!

Scripture: *"The Lord is near to those who have a broken heart, and saves such as have a contrite spirit.* (Psalm 34:18)

14. Prayer for Strength to Resist Negative Influences

Prayer: Lord, I ask for Your strength to resist every negative influence that seeks to pull me away from Your purpose. I clothe myself in Your armor, and with fire, I strike down every temptation and negative influence. Thunder of heaven, empower me to stand firm and not yield to the pressures of the enemy! I declare that I am strong in the Lord and in the power of His might!

Scripture: *"Finally, my brethren, be strong in the Lord and in the power of His might. Put on the whole armor of God, that you may be able to stand against the wiles of the devil."* (Ephesians 6:10-11)

Prayer Points from Samuel's Life:

1. Prayer for a Heart to Hear God

Prayer: Lord, I pray that my child will have a heart that is sensitive to Your voice, just like Samuel. Help them to discern Your will and respond with obedience.
Scripture: *"Now the Lord came and stood and called as at other times, 'Samuel! Samuel!' And Samuel answered, 'Speak, for Your servant hears.'"* (1 Samuel 3:10)

2. Prayer for Dedication to God

Prayer: Father, I dedicate my child to You today. May they grow in Your presence, fulfilling the purpose for which You created them.
Scripture: *" 'For this child I prayed, and the Lord has granted me my petition which I asked of Him. Therefore I also have lent him to the Lord; as long as he lives he shall be lent to the Lord.' So they worshiped the Lord there."* (1 Samuel 1:27-28)

3. Prayer for Faithfulness and Integrity

Prayer: God, instill in my child a spirit of faithfulness and integrity. May they always honor You and serve with a pure heart.
Scripture : *"Only fear the Lord, and serve Him in truth with all your heart; for consider what great things He has done for you."* (1 Samuel 12:24)

4. Prayer for Wisdom and Discernment

Prayer: Lord, grant my child wisdom and discernment to see beyond the outward appearances and to make choices that align with Your purpose.
Scripture : *"But the Lord said to Samuel, 'Do not look at his appearance or at his physical stature, because I have refused him. For the Lord does not see as man sees; for man looks at the outward appearance, but the Lord looks at the heart'"* (1 Samuel 16:7)

5. Prayer for Courage to Stand for Righteousness

Prayer: Father, empower my child to stand firm in righteousness, even when it is unpopular. May they be bold in declaring Your truth.
Scripture: *"So Samuel said: 'Has the Lord as great delight in burnt offerings and sacrifices, as in obeying the voice of the Lord? Behold, to obey is better than sacrifice, and to heed than the fat of rams'" (1 Samuel 15:22).*

6. Prayer for Divine Guidance

Prayer : Lord, guide my child in all their ways. May they trust in You with all their heart and lean not on their own understanding.
Scripture : *"Trust in the Lord with all your heart, And lean not on your own understanding; In all your ways acknowledge Him, and He shall direct your paths."* (Proverbs 3:5-6)

7. Prayer for Protection from Negative Influences

Prayer : Heavenly Father, protect my child from harmful influences and surround them with godly friendships that will encourage them in their walk with You.
Scripture: *"For He shall give His angels charge over you, To keep you in all your ways."* (Psalm 91:11)

8. Prayer for a Passion for Prayer and Worship

Prayer : Lord, ignite in my child a passion for prayer and worship. May they seek You earnestly and draw closer to You every day.
Scripture : *"And Samuel took a suckling lamb and offered it as a whole burnt offering to the Lord. Then Samuel cried out to the Lord for Israel, and the Lord answered him."* (1 Samuel 7:9)

Day 16: Thou Can NOT Be Barren

1. Prayer for Divine Intervention

Prayer : Heavenly Father, just as You remembered Rachel and opened her womb, I call upon You to intervene in my situation. Let every barrier to conception be consumed by Your fire in the name of Jesus!
Scripture : *"Then God remembered Rachel, and God listened to her and opened her womb."* (Genesis 30:22)

2. Prayer to Break Curses of Barrenness

Prayer : Lord, I decree and declare that I shall not be barren. I break every curse of barrenness and every negative word spoken over my womb. Let the fire of God consume these curses and turn them to ashes in the name of Jesus!
Scripture : *"You shall be blessed above all peoples; there shall not be a male or female barren among you or among your livestock."* (Deuteronomy 7:14)

3. Prayer for Restoration of Reproductive Health

Prayer : Father, restore my reproductive health in the name of Jesus. Let the fire of the Holy Ghost purge every illness, blockage, or condition causing barrenness in my life!
Scripture : *"For I will restore health to you and heal you of your wounds,' says the Lord, 'because they called you an outcast, saying: "This is Zion; no one seeks her."'* (Jeremiah 30:17)

4. Prayer to Uproot Spirit of Barrenness

Prayer Point: Every spirit of barrenness planted in my life, I uproot you by the fire of God! You shall no longer hold sway over my destiny. Be consumed by the fire of the Holy Spirit in the name of Jesus!
Scripture : *"But He answered and said, "Every plant which My heavenly Father has not planted will be uprooted.* (Matthew 15:13)

5. Prayer for the Fire of God to Purify

Prayer : O God, send Your refining fire upon my womb and purify it. Let every impurity, every demonic influence, and every obstacle be burned away, so that I may conceive and bear children in the name of Jesus!

Scripture : *"But who can endure the day of His coming? And who can stand when He appears? For He is like a refiner's fire and like launderer's' soap. He will sit as a refiner and a purifier of silver; He will purify the sons of Levi, and purge them as gold and silver, that they may offer to the Lord an offering in righteousness."*(Malachi 3:2-3)

6. Prayer for Faith and Expectation

Prayer : Lord, just as Sarah received strength to conceive when she was past age, I pray for a supernatural infusion of faith and expectation. Let the fire of God ignite my hope and cause my womb to be fruitful, in Jesus' name!

Scripture: *" By faith Sarah herself also received strength to conceive seed, and she bore a child when she was past the age, because she judged Him faithful who had promised."* (Hebrews 11:11)

7. Prayer Against Negative Influences

Prayer : I cancel every negative declaration, every word of discouragement spoken over my life and womb. Let the fire of God consume these words and turn them to dust, as I declare my fruitfulness in the name of Jesus!

Scripture : *"Death and life are in the power of the tongue, and those who love it will eat its fruit."* (Proverbs 18:21)

8. Prayer for Divine Connection

Prayer: For with God, nothing shall be impossible! I pray that You connect me with every divine helper and resource I need for my journey to motherhood. Let every blockage preventing these connections be consumed by Your fire in the name of Jesus!
Scripture : *"For with God nothing will be impossible."* (Luke 1:37)

9. Prayer for Generational Blessings

Prayer: I decree and declare that there shall be no barrenness in my family line! I call upon the fire of God to burn away every generational curse of barrenness and replace it with a blessing of fruitfulness in the name of Jesus!
Scripture : *"No one shall suffer miscarriage or be barren in your land; I will fulfill the number of your days."* (Exodus 23:26)

10. Prayer for Spiritual Growth and Preparation

Prayer : I speak forth life into my womb! Let the fire of God prepare me spiritually and emotionally for the gift of motherhood. May my heart and mind be aligned with Your purpose, Lord!
Scripture : *" 'Sing, O barren, you who have not borne! Break forth into singing, and cry aloud, you who have not labored with child! For more are the children of the desolate than the children of the married woman,' says the Lord."* (Isaiah 54:1)

11. Breaking Generational Curses

Prayer: Any curse of barrenness from my family line, I break you by the blood of Jesus! I declare that I shall bear children!

12. Divine Intervention

Prayer: O Lord, intervene in my situation as You did for Sarah and Hannah. Let Your power bring forth life in my womb!

13. Angelic Assistance

Prayer: Father, send Your angels to remove every obstacle to my conception and let them fight against every spiritual hindrance!

14. Divine Timing

Prayer: I declare that my time for fruitfulness has come. Every delay, I command you to cease in the name of Jesus!

15. Prophetic Declaration

Prayer: Just as the Shunamite woman received a prophetic word, I receive my word of fruitfulness today. I decree that my womb is blessed!

16. Filling the Empty Spaces

Prayer: Every void in my life, be filled with the blessings of children. I command barrenness to depart from my life!

17. Restoration of Fertility

Prayer: Every spirit of barrenness, I cast you out of my life and declare restoration to my fertility in the name of Jesus!

18. Praise and Thanksgiving

Prayer: I thank You, Lord, for my miracle children. I believe that I will soon testify of Your goodness!

19. Praying for children and the eventual fulfillment of their desires through faith and divine intervention.

Here are some notable examples:

1. Sarah (Genesis 11:30; 21:1-7)
   - Anguish: Sarah was barren for many years, which caused her distress and led her to give Hagar to Abraham as a concubine to bear a child (Genesis 16). The delay in the promise of a child caused tension in her marriage.
   - Overcoming: God intervened, and at the age of 90, Sarah bore Isaac, fulfilling His promise. She laughed at the miraculous news and named her son Isaac, meaning "laughter."

Prayer: Father, just as You turned the laughter of Sarah into joy, turn my barrenness into fruitfulness. I declare that my season of joy has come!

2. Rebekah (Genesis 25:21)
   - Anguish: Rebekah was barren for many years, and her husband Isaac prayed for her. Her barrenness caused distress not only for her but also for Isaac, who longed for children.
   - Overcoming: Isaac's prayers were answered, and Rebekah conceived twins, Esau and Jacob, after she sought God's guidance regarding her pregnancy.

Prayer: Lord, hear my cry and answer my prayers like You did for Isaac and Rebekah. Grant me the desires of my heart!

3. Rachel (Genesis 30:1-2)
   - Anguish: Rachel's barrenness caused jealousy and rivalry with her sister Leah, who bore many children. Rachel's anguish led her to demand children from Jacob, saying, "Give me children, or else I die."
   - Overcoming: After much prayer and anguish, God remembered Rachel and

Prayer: I thank You, Lord, for my miracle children. I believe that I will soon testify of Your goodness!

Day 17: Purple Linen

Resources flow freely to me, and I operate in the overflow of God's blessings. I am open to the new strategies God is revealing to me. I embrace growth and success, and every limitation is removed by God's power.

1. Heavenly Father, I come to You seeking financial wisdom and guidance in my life.
Scripture: *"The plans of the diligent lead to profit as surely as haste leads to poverty."* (Proverbs 21:5)

2. Lord, help me to manage my resources wisely and to be a good steward of what You have entrusted to me.
Scripture: *"Each of you should give what you have decided in your heart to give, not reluctantly or under compulsion."* (2 Corinthians 9:7)

3. Grant me the insight to recognize and seize opportunities for financial growth.
Scripture: *"In all your ways acknowledge Him, and He will make your paths straight."* (Proverbs 3:6)

4. Help me to break free from any financial bondage or past mistakes that hinder my progress.
Scripture: *"You will know the truth, and the truth will set you free."* (John 8:32)

5. Fill me with a spirit of diligence and perseverance, so that I may work hard and achieve my goals.
Scripture: *"Whatever you do, work at it with all your heart, as working for the Lord."* (Colossians 3:23)

6. Lord, bless the work of my hands and multiply my efforts as I strive to provide for my needs and those of my family.
Scripture: *"The blessing of the Lord brings wealth, without painful toil for it."* (Proverbs 10:22)

7. Help me to trust in Your provision and to seek first Your kingdom and righteousness.

Scripture: *"But seek first His kingdom and His righteousness, and all these things will be given to you as well."* (Matthew 6:33)

8. Thank You for Your faithfulness and for the abundance You provide. I believe You are opening doors for my financial rise.

Scripture: *"And my God will meet all your needs according to the riches of His glory in Christ Jesus."* (Philippians 4:19)

Prayer Points for Financial Abundance:

9. Financial Breakthrough

Prayer: Heavenly Father, I come before You, seeking a financial breakthrough. Every financial bondage and limitation in my life, I command you to be broken now in the name of Jesus!

10. Prayer for Divine Opportunities

Prayer: Lord, I pray that You open doors of opportunity for me in my career and business. Let divine connections lead me to places of wealth and abundance, in Jesus' name.

11. Favor in Financial Matters
Prayer: O God, grant me favor with my employers, clients, and customers. May my work and efforts be rewarded abundantly, and may I find favor in every financial transaction, in Jesus' name.

12. Against Financial Setbacks
Prayer: In the name of Jesus, I come against every spirit of setback and failure in my finances. I declare that every barrier that has hindered my financial progress is removed, and I move forward into abundance.

13. Increase in Income
Prayer: Father, I ask for an increase in my income. Whether through my job, investments, or business, I declare that my income will multiply, and I will have more than enough to meet my needs and share with others.

14. Wise Stewardship
Prayer: Lord, help me to be a good steward of the resources You have blessed me with. Teach me to manage my finances wisely, that I may save, invest, and give generously, in Jesus' name.

15. Breaking Curses of Poverty

Prayer: I break every curse of poverty and lack over my life and family. I declare that I am free from generational curses that hinder financial prosperity. I am blessed to be a blessing!

16. Financial Wisdom

Prayer: Father, grant me wisdom in my financial decisions. Help me to recognize good opportunities and to avoid pitfalls. May I make decisions that lead to prosperity and success.

17. Divine Provision

Prayer: O Lord, I trust in Your provision. I ask that You supply all my needs according to Your riches in glory. Let Your abundance flow into my life, providing for every need I have.

18. The Anointing to Create Wealth

Prayer: I declare the anointing to create wealth upon my life. May the ideas, strategies, and creativity flow in me, leading to profitable ventures and success in all my endeavors.

19. Protection of Wealth

Prayer: I plead the blood of Jesus over my finances and possessions. I declare that no thief, no spirit of loss, and no form of attack shall come against my financial prosperity.

20. God's Guidance:

Prayer: Heavenly Father, guide me in my financial journey. Show me where to invest, how to save, and how to grow my wealth in ways that honor You and bless others.

Day 17: Mantled for Wealth

21. Divine Connection

Prayer: Father, I decree and declare that every divine connection ordained for my financial breakthrough will locate me now. Let the right people come into my life, those who will lift me and align with my destiny in the name of Jesus!

22. The Anointing to Prosper

Prayer: Lord, I pray for the anointing to prosper in every area of my life. Let Your divine favor rest upon my hands, that whatever I touch shall prosper and yield fruit, in the name of Jesus!

23. Divine Strategies

Prayer: Holy Spirit, grant me strategies for financial increase. Open my eyes to opportunities that I have overlooked. Give me the wisdom to make decisions that align with Your purpose for my life, in Jesus' name!

24. Breakthrough in Business:

Prayer: O God, I declare a season of divine breakthroughs in my business. Every barrier that has hindered my success is dismantled now. Let unusual favor and financial opportunities pursue me, in Jesus' name!

25. Generational Wealth:

Prayer: Father, I stand in the gap for my family. I declare that every curse of poverty and lack is broken. I claim generational wealth and abundance that will flow through my lineage, in the name of Jesus!

26. Abundant Harvest:

Prayer: Lord, I speak to the seeds I have sown, both financially and spiritually. I declare that they will yield a bountiful harvest.

Every limitation on my harvest is lifted now, in Jesus' name!

27. Favor in Financial Transactions
Prayer: Heavenly Father, grant me favor in all my financial transactions. Let every negotiation, deal, and agreement be saturated with Your divine favor. I declare that I will not miss any opportunity that You have ordained for me!

28. Financial Restoration
Prayer: God of restoration, I ask for the restoration of lost opportunities and finances. Every penny that has been lost or stolen, I command it to be returned to me now in the name of Jesus!

29. Supernatural Provision
Prayer: Lord, I ask for Your supernatural provision in my life. Just as You provided for the Israelites in the wilderness, provide for me in unexpected ways and open doors of abundance, in Jesus' name!

30. The Spirit of Excellence
Prayer: Father, I pray for a spirit of excellence to rest upon me in my work and endeavors. Help me to deliver quality that attracts clients and customers, leading to abundant financial rewards, in Jesus' name!

31. Financial Limitations:
Prayer: In the name of Jesus, I break every limitation and restriction on my finances. I declare that I am not confined to the system of this world; I operate under the economy of Heaven!

32. Wisdom in Investments:
Prayer: O Lord, grant me wisdom to make profitable investments. Teach me to discern opportunities that align with Your will for my life, ensuring that my finances grow and multiply for Your glory!

33. Favor in Employment
Prayer: Father, I pray for favor in my current job or any job I am seeking. Let my skills and talents shine forth, attracting recognition and promotion in the workplace, in Jesus' name!

34. Breaking Financial Curses
Prayer: I declare every financial curse from my family line is broken by the blood of Jesus. I am a child of the King, and I refuse to live in lack or poverty. Abundance is my portion!

35. Gratefulness and Generosity
Prayer: Lord, instill in me a heart of gratitude and generosity. Help me to understand that as I give, I shall also receive. May my hands be open to bless others, and may Your blessings flow into my life abundantly!

36. Joy and Contentment
Prayer: Lord, help me to find joy and contentment in what I have. May my desire for wealth be balanced with gratitude for Your blessings and a heart to share with those in need.

37. Breaking the Spirit of Greed
Prayer: I renounce the spirit of greed and covetousness in my life. Help me to have a heart that is generous and willing to give, knowing that as I give, I shall also receive.

38. Overflowing Abundance
Prayer: I declare that I am a candidate for overflowing abundance. May my cup run over with blessings, and may I have enough to bless my family, community, and the work of Your kingdom.
Scripture: *"Iron sharpens iron, so one person sharpens another."* (Proverbs 27:17)

39. Divine Creativity

Prayer: Heavenly Father, I come before You today asking for Your divine creativity to flow through me. Open my mind and heart to receive innovative ideas and witty inventions that will bring glory to Your name and solutions to the world around me. In Jesus' name, Amen.

40. Divine Insight

Prayer: Lord, grant me insight and revelation that goes beyond human understanding. Help me to see opportunities for innovation where others see obstacles. I declare that I will be a vessel for Your creative power in the marketplace and beyond!

41. Ideas That Transform

Prayer: O God, I pray for ideas that will transform my life and the lives of others. Let my inventions and creations be solutions to the problems that plague our society. Use me to bring about change and improvement in every area I touch.

42. Favor in Implementation

Prayer: Father, as You give me witty inventions, I ask for favor in their implementation. Surround me with the right people, resources, and opportunities to bring my ideas to fruition. Let nothing hinder my progress in the name of Jesus!

44. The Spirit of Innovation

Prayer: Holy Spirit, breathe upon me a spirit of innovation. Help me to think outside the box and develop solutions that reflect Your wisdom and understanding. I declare that I will operate in creativity and excellence!

45. Networking and Partnerships
Prayer: Lord, connect me with like-minded individuals and partners who share my vision for innovation. May our collaborations yield fruitful results, and may we inspire one another to reach new heights of creativity and achievement!

46. Protection Against Stagnation
Prayer: In the name of Jesus, I bind every spirit of stagnation and mediocrity that seeks to hold me back from achieving my creative potential. I declare that I am free to explore new ideas and step into the fullness of my calling!

47. Wisdom in Execution
Prayer: Heavenly Father, grant me the wisdom to execute my ideas effectively. Help me develop plans and strategies that align with Your will and lead to success. I declare that my efforts will be fruitful and multiply!

48. Courage to Step Out
Prayer: Lord, give me the courage to step out in faith with the ideas You have given me. Help me to overcome fear and doubt, knowing that You are with me every step of the way. I will not shrink back, for I am empowered by Your Spirit!

49. Continuous Inspiration
Prayer: O God, may I continually be inspired by Your creativity. Let me seek You in prayer and meditation, drawing from the well of Your wisdom to sustain my creative endeavors. I thank You for the flow of ideas that will come as I abide in You!

Day 18: Marital Shield

1. Divine Protection

Prayer: Heavenly Father, I come before You to seek divine protection over my marriage. Shield my spouse and me from every attack of the enemy. Let no weapon formed against us prosper.

Scripture: *"No weapon forged against you will prevail, and you will refute every tongue that accuses you."* (Isaiah 54:17)

2. Unity and Love

Prayer: Lord, unite our hearts and minds in love and understanding. Help us to communicate openly and support one another in all things. May our love grow stronger every day.

Scripture: *"And over all these virtues put on love, which binds them all together in perfect unity."* (Colossians 3:14)

3. Divine Wisdom

Prayer: Father, grant us wisdom to navigate the challenges of life together. May we make decisions that honor You and strengthen our marriage.

Scripture: *"If any of you lacks wisdom, let him ask of God, who gives to all liberally and without reproach, and it will be given to him."* (James 1:5)

4. Warfare Prayer Against Divisive Spirits

Prayer: In the name of Jesus, I bind and cast out every spirit of division and strife that seeks to invade my marriage. I declare peace and harmony in our home.

Scripture: *"A house divided against itself cannot stand."* (Mark 3:25)

5. Divine Protection

Prayer: Lord, surround my marriage with Your hedge of protection. Shield us from every attack of the enemy, both seen and unseen.

6. Unity
Prayer: Father, let every spirit of division and misunderstanding be cast out. Bind our hearts together in perfect harmony.

7. Restoration
Prayer: Lord, restore any lost love or intimacy in our relationship. Renew our hearts and rekindle the fire of our love.

8. Wisdom
Prayer: Holy Spirit, grant us wisdom to navigate challenges and decisions together. Help us communicate effectively and understand each other deeply.

9. Fruitfulness
Prayer: In the name of Jesus, I declare our marriage fruitful in every aspect—emotionally, spiritually, and physically. Let our union bring glory to Your name.

10. Negative Influences
Prayer: Lord, expose and remove every negative influence and person that seeks to disrupt our marriage.

11. Financial Blessings
Prayer: Heavenly Father, bless the work of our hands. Provide for our needs and enable us to thrive together.

12. Spiritual Warfare
Prayer: Father, we take authority over every spirit of conflict and strife.

13. Peace in Our Home
Prayer: For we wrestle not against flesh and blood, but against principalities, against powers, against the rulers of the darkness of this world, against spiritual wickedness in high places. (Ephesians 6:12)

14. Mutual Understanding
Prayer: Lord, grant us wisdom and understanding in our dealings with each other

Scripture: *"If any of you lacks wisdom, let him ask of God, who gives to all liberally and without reproach, and it will be given to him."*(James 1:5).

15. Faithfulness
Prayer: Heavenly Father, help us to remain faithful to one another as you are faithful to us.

Scripture: *"No temptation has overtaken you except such as is common to man; but God is faithful, who will not allow you to be tempted beyond what you are able, but with the temptation will also make the way of escape, that you may be able to bear it."*(1 Corinthians 10:13)

16. Healing of Past Wounds
Prayer: Heavenly Father, heal any past wounds or traumas that affect our marriage. Help us to forgive one another and to move forward in love and trust.

Scripture: *"He heals the brokenhearted and binds up their wounds."* (Psalm 147:3)

17. Godly Counsel and Mentorship
Prayer: Lord, surround us with godly mentors and couples who can offer us wise counsel and support in our marriage journey.

Scripture: *"Without counsel plans fail, but with many advisers, they succeed."* (Proverbs 15:22)

18. Father, please grant every home victory over all the attacks of the enemy, in Jesus' name.

19. Father, please open the wombs of all Your children that are married and are seeking Your face for fruitfulness, in Jesus' name.

20: Powerful Declarations on your Marriage:

Confession: I confess today that God's blessings will saturate my marriage, filling it with joy, wisdom, and enduring love, in the mighty name of Jesus

I decree and declare that my marriage is a blessed institution, overflowing with the joy and companionship God intended, in the mighty name of Jesus.

I decree and declare, let God's wisdom floods my home, guiding me, my spouse, and future generations, in the mighty name of Jesus.

I decree and declare that every lack in my marriage is replenished with God's abundant goodness, just like the wine at Cana, in the mighty name of Jesus.

I decree and declare that storms may come, but Your peace reigns supreme, calming and restoring my marriage, in the mighty name of Jesus.

I decree and declare that Godly children shall arise from blessed our homes, serving You with purpose and dedication, in the mighty name of Jesus.

I declare marital breakthroughs flow freely, leading Your children to loving, fulfilling unions, in the mighty name of Jesus.

Day 19: Fight to Possess

1. Divine Strategy
Prayer: Lord, give me divine strategy for the battles ahead. Just as You gave Israel insight to engage in warfare, grant me the wisdom to know how to fight and win. I receive divine direction for every battle in my life in Jesus' name!

2. Remove Limitations
Prayer: In the name of Jesus, every limitation placed on my advancement, I break you now! No force of the enemy will hinder my forward movement. I declare acceleration and divine speed into my destiny in Jesus' name!

3. Possession by Fire
Prayer: Father, I possess my inheritance by fire! Every delay is consumed by the fire of the Holy Spirit. I claim my breakthrough, my blessings, and my divine portion, and I declare nothing will stop me from taking what is mine in Jesus' name!

4. Overcoming Generational Battles
Prayer: I break every generational battle that seeks to keep me in bondage. By the blood of Jesus, I cancel every curse and ancestral stronghold that has held my family captive. I declare my freedom to possess all that God has ordained for me!

5. Faith and Boldness
Prayer: Lord, I receive boldness to step into my destiny. Fear will no longer hold me back. I declare that I walk in courage and faith, taking hold of every opportunity You have placed before me in the name of Jesus!

6. Divine Empowerment

Prayer: Father, empower me to war with the prophecies spoken over my life. I activate the strength to engage in spiritual warfare, knowing that the battle is already won. I will see the fulfillment of Your promises in my life!

7. Advance Without Delay

Prayer: Lord, I refuse to delay any longer. I move forward with divine speed, crossing every boundary and breaking every limitation. I declare that now is my time to take possession of my inheritance in Jesus' name!

8. God's Intervention in Battle

Prayer: Father, just as You intervened for Israel, intervene in my battles today. Let Your mighty hand bring supernatural victory, and let my enemies be scattered before me in the name of Jesus!

9. Complete Victory

Prayer: I declare complete victory over every battle in my life. No territory will be left unconquered, and no blessing will be left untouched. I walk in total dominion and authority, claiming every blessing that has been promised to me in Jesus' name!

Scriptural References

- Deuteronomy 2:24 – Possess and engage in battle.
- Joshua 1:3 – Every place where you set your foot will be yours.
- Isaiah 54:17 – No weapon formed against you shall prosper.
- Romans 8:37 – We are more than conquerors through Him who loved us.

1. Every evil gathering against me, be scattered by the thunder fire of God, in the name of Jesus.

2. O Lord, let Your fire destroy every evil list containing my name, in the name of Jesus.

3. All failures of the past, be converted to success, in Jesus name.

4. O Lord, let the former rain, the latter rain, and Your blessings pour down on me now, in the name of Jesus

5. O Lord, let all the failure mechanisms of the enemy designed against my success be frustrated, in the name of Jesus.

6. I receive power from on high and I paralyze all the powers of darkness that are diverting my blessings, in the name of Jesus.

7. Beginning from this day, I employ the services of the angels of God to open unto me every door of opportunity and breakthroughs, in the name of Jesus.

8. I will not go around in circles again, I will make progress, in the name of Jesus.

9. I shall not build for another to inhabit and I shall not plant for another to eat, in the name of Jesus.

10. I paralyze the powers of the emptier concerning my handiwork, in the name of Jesus.

11. Every locust, caterpillar and palmer-worm assigned to eat the fruit of my labor, be roasted by the fire of God, in Jesus name.

12. The enemy shall not spoil my testimonies, in the name of Jesus.

13. I reject every backward journey, in the name of Jesus.

14. I paralyze every strongman attached to any area of my life, in the name of Jesus.

15. Let every agent of shame fashioned to work against my life be paralyzed, in the name of Jesus.

16. I paralyze the activities of household wickedness over my life, in the name of Jesus.

17. I quench every strange fire emanating from evil tongues against me, in the name of Jesus.

18. O Lord, give me power for maximum achievement, in the name of Jesus.

19. O Lord, give me comforting authority to achieve my goal, in the name of Jesus.

20. O Lord, fortify me with Your power, in the name of Jesus.

21. Every curse of profitless hard work upon my life, break, in the name of Jesus. (Lay your right hand on your head while praying this prayer point.)

22. Every curse of non-achievement upon my life, break, in the name of Jesus. (Lay your right hand on your head while praying this prayer point.)

23. Every curse of backwardness upon my life, break, in the name of Jesus. (Lay your right hand on your head while praying this prayer point.)

24. I paralyze every spirit of disobedience in my life, in Jesus name.

25. I refuse to disobey the voice of God, in the name of Jesus.

26. Every root of rebellion in my life, be uprooted, in Jesus name.

27. Fountain of rebellion in my life, dry up, in the name of Jesus.

28. Contrary powers fueling rebellion in my life, die, in Jesus name.

29. Every inspiration of witchcraft in my family, be destroyed, in the name of Jesus.

30. Blood of Jesus, blot out every evil mark of witchcraft in my life, in the name of Jesus.

31. Every garment put upon me by witchcraft, be torn to pieces, in the name of Jesus.

32. Angels of God, begin to pursue my household enemies, let their ways be dark and slippery, in the name of Jesus.

33. O Lord, confuse my household enemies and turn them against themselves, in the name of Jesus.

34. Break every evil unconscious agreement with household enemies concerning my miracles, in the name of Jesus.

35. Household witchcraft, fall down and die, in the name of Jesus.

36. O Lord, drag all my household wickedness to the dead sea and bury them there, in the name of Jesus.

Day 20: Doors of Destiny

Scripture:
"I have set before you an open door that no one can shut." (Revelation 3:8)
"I will place on his shoulder the key to the house of David; what he opens, no one can shut." (Isaiah 22:22)

1. Grace for Opportunities
Prayer: Grant me the grace to recognize divine opportunities

Give me the wisdom to discern the right doors to walk through

Scripture: *"Of the sons of Issachar who had understanding of the times, to know what Israel ought to do, their chiefs were two hundred; and all their brethren were at their command."* (1 Chronicles 12:32)

2. Breakthrough from Limitations
Prayer: Every limitation standing before my open doors, be broken in Jesus' name.

Every hindrance to my opportunities, be removed by the power of God

Scripture: *"I will go before you and make the crooked places straight; I will break in pieces the gates of bronze and cut the bars of iron."* (Isaiah 45:2)

3. Divine Favor
Prayer: Lord, let Your favor surround me and open uncommon doors

May I find favor with the right people who hold the keys to my opportunities

Scripture: *"For You, O Lord, will bless the righteous; with favor You will surround him as with a shield."* (Psalm 5:12)

4. Supernatural Speed

Prayer: I declare supernatural speed as I enter open doors of greatness

May every delay over my opportunities be lifted in Jesus' name

Scripture: *"Then the hand of the Lord came upon Elijah; and he girded up his loins and ran ahead of Ahab to the entrance of Jezreel."* (1 Kings 18:46)

5. Access to New Territories

Prayer: Father, open doors to new territories, new lands, and greater influence

Expand my boundaries and enlarge my territory.

Scripture: *"Enlarge the place of your tent, and let them stretch out the curtains of your dwellings; do not spare; lengthen your cords, and strengthen your stakes."* (Isaiah 54:2)

6. Restoration of Lost Opportunities

Prayer: I call forth restoration of every lost or missed opportunity

Lord, redeem the time and restore what the enemy has stolen.

Scripture: *"So I will restore to you the years that the swarming locust has eaten, the crawling locust,t he consuming locust, and the chewing locust, my great army which I sent among you.*(Joel 2:25)

7. Boldness to Enter Open Doors

Prayer: Grant me the boldness to walk through the doors You have opened for me

Remove every fear and hesitation that would keep me from my breakthroughs

Scripture: *"Have I not commanded you? Be strong and of good courage; do not be afraid, nor be dismayed, for the Lord your God is with you wherever you go."* 111 (Joshua 1:9)

8. Breaking Spiritual Barriers

Prayer: Every spiritual gate of opposition, be destroyed by fire

I decree that no demonic force will close the doors that God has opened.

Scripture: *And I will give you the keys of the kingdom of heaven, and whatever you bind on earth will be bound in heaven, and whatever you loose on earth will be loosed in heaven.*"(Matthew 16:19)

9. Divine Timing

Prayer: Let every door be opened at the appointed time according to Your will

Grant me patience and discernment to recognize Your perfect timing

Scripture: *To everything there is a season, a time for every purpose under heaven* (Ecclesiastes 3:1)

10. Protection Over Open Doors

Prayer: Lord, protect the doors You've opened for me from any enemy attacks

Seal every opportunity with Your divine protection and grace

Scripture: *The Lord shall preserve you from all evil; He shall preserve your soul. The Lord shall preserve your going out and your coming in from this time forth, and even forevermore.*(Psalm 121:7-8)

11. Divine Wisdom for Opportunities

Prayer: Grant me wisdom to manage and maximize every open door

Help me steward opportunities with integrity and excellence

Scripture: *"If any of you lacks wisdom, let him ask of God, who gives to all liberally and without reproach, and it will be given to him."* (James 1:5)

12. Supernatural Increase
Prayer: Lord, open doors of supernatural increase and abundance

Let Your blessings overflow in my life as I enter these new opportunities

 Scripture: *The blessing of the Lord makes one rich, and He adds no sorrow with it.* (Proverbs 10:22)

13. Grace to Sustain Open Doors
Prayer: Father, grant me the grace to sustain and manage the doors You have opened

Scripture:*"And to the angel of the church in Philadelphia write, 'These things says He who is holy, He who is true, He who has the key of David, He who opens and no one shuts, and shuts and no one opens: I know your works. See, I have set before you an open door, and no one can shut it; for you have a little strength, have kept My word, and have not denied My name.'"* **(Revelation 3:7-8)**

14. Let me never squander any opportunity that You have given.

15. I stand on the platform of Calvary and decree my breakthroughs today, in the name of Jesus.

16. Every power of darkness fueling my problems, be arrested, in the name of Jesus.

17. Every source of failure in my life, I sentence you to death, in the name of Jesus.

18. Thou fountain of sickness in my body, I kill you, in the name of Jesus.

19. Every trespassing power that is harassing my destiny, die, in the name of Jesus.

20. Thunder power of God, kill infirmity in my body, in the name of Jesus.

21. Let the bullet from heaven kill every serpent of death assigned against me, in the name of Jesus.

22. Let the killing force of the Almighty arise and kill my problems, in the name of Jesus.

23. Every snake anointed by the enemy against me, die, in the name of Jesus.

24. Thou killing incantations, backfire now, in the name of Jesus.

25. I command every stronghold of Satan in my body to die, in the name of Jesus.

26. Every root of captivity in my life, die, in the name of Jesus.

27. Earthquake of deliverance, begin your rage on my behalf, in the name of Jesus.

28. Deliverance anger of the Lord, rage for my sake, in the name of Jesus.

29. Every ancient prison door in my family line, break, in the name of Jesus.

30. Communal bondage limiting my laughter, die, in the name of Jesus.

31. Liberation explosion, manifest in my life, in the name of Jesus.

32. Personal spiritual chains upon my life, break, in the name of Jesus.

33. Ancestral spiritual chains upon my life, break, in the name of Jesus.

34. Earthquake of the Lord's deliverance, quake by fire for my sake, in the name of Jesus.

35. O Lord, give me the key to foundational deliverance, in the name of Jesus.

36. O Lord, renew my youth like Eagle, in the name of Jesus.

37. Every destiny vulture, vomit my breakthroughs, in the name of Jesus.

38. Every satanic agenda for my destiny, die, in the name of Jesus.

39. Negative inheritance, die, in the name of Jesus.

40. Every evil power that pursued my parents, release me, in the name of Jesus.

41. Fire of God, separate me from my inherited darkness, in the name of Jesus.

42. Let the confidence of the wicked over my life be broken, in the name of Jesus.

43. I reject every satanic re-arrangement of my destiny, in the name of Jesus.

44. Thou power of God, uproot wicked plantations from my life, in the name of Jesus.

45. Father, I thank you for your mercies over my life, it is because of your mercies that I am not consumed, thank you father, in Jesus name.

46. O Lord, remember me for good and open the book of remembrance for me, in Jesus name.

47. I cancel and scatter every demonic activities in my life, in the name of Jesus.

48. By the blood of Jesus Christ, I reverse every damage done to my life from birth, in Jesus name.

49. By the blood of Jesus Christ, I close every doors which the devil enters through to afflict me in my life, in Jesus name.

50. O Lord, restore the wasted years of my life, in Jesus name.

51. I take back every single territory held by the enemy in my life, in the name of Jesus.

52. I break out and deliver myself from every evil prison, in the name of Jesus.

53. Every foundational infirmity in my life, depart from my life now, in Jesus name.

54. I will reign as king over my circumstances, in the name of Jesus.

55. Every evil family curse, be destroyed in my life, in Jesus name.

56. Help me O Lord to recognize Your voice, in Jesus name.

57. O Lord, Open the eyes of my understanding, in Jesus name

58. I throw off every burden of worry in my life, in the name of Jesus.

59. I refuse to be entangled with evil thoughts, in the name of Jesus.

60. Every satanic road block hindering my progress, scatter, in Jesus name.

61. My spiritual climate, send terror to the camp of the enemies, in the name of Jesus.

62. O Lord, release me from every evil words and evil silences, in Jesus name

63. Every witchcraft power assigned against my life and marriage, receive the thunder and lighting of God, in the name of Jesus.

64. I release myself from any inherited bondage, in the name of Jesus.

65. I release myself from the grip of any problem transferred into my life from the womb, in the name of Jesus.

66. I break and loose myself from every inherited evil covenant, in the name of Jesus.

67. I take authority over and order the binding of every strongman in every department of my life, in the name of Jesus.

68. Good doors of financial breakthroughs, open unto me now, in the name of Jesus.

69. Good doors of business / career breakthroughs, open unto me, in the name of Jesus.

70. Good doors of marital breakthrough, open unto me now, in the name of Jesus.

71. O God arise and network me with my destiny helpers, in the name of Jesus.

72. Holy Ghost, empower me to recognize divine opportunities, in the name of Jesus.

73. Lord Jesus let your anointing set me aside for greatness and Divine upliftment.

Day 21: Thanksgiving for Possessing your Possession

1. **Prayer:** Heavenly Father, I come before You with a grateful heart, thanking You for all the blessings You have poured into my life.
Scripture: *"Every good gift and every perfect gift is from above."* (James 1:17)

2. **Prayer:** Lord, I thank You for the possessions and resources You have entrusted to me. I recognize they are a reflection of Your grace.
Scripture: *"The earth is the Lord's, and everything in it."* (Psalm 24:1)

3. **Prayer**: Thank You for granting me the ability to work and provide for myself and my family.
Scripture: *"You shall eat the fruit of the labor of your hands; you shall be blessed, and it shall be well with you."* (Psalm 128:2)

4. **Prayer**: I praise You for the opportunities You have given me to grow and prosper in my endeavors.
Scripture: *"And I will make you prosper; you will be fruitful and multiply."* (Genesis 1:28)

5. **Prayer**: Lord, I ask for Your forgiveness for the times I have fallen short. Cleanse my heart and renew my spirit.
Scripture: *"If we confess our sins, He is faithful and just and will forgive us our sins and purify us from all unrighteousness."* (1 John 1:9)

6. **Prayer**: Father, grant me the courage to face my failures and the wisdom to understand the lessons they bring.
Scripture: *"And we know that in all things God works for the good of those who love Him, who have been called according to His purpose."* (Romans 8:28)

7. **Prayer**: Lord, help me to rise above discouragement and despair. Fill me with hope and a renewed sense of purpose.
Scripture: *"But those who hope in the Lord will renew their strength. They will soar on wings like eagles."* (Isaiah 40:31)

8. **Prayer**: Father, I pray for resilience to keep pressing forward, no matter how many times I stumble. Strengthen my faith in You.
Scripture: *"I can do all things through Christ who strengthens me."* (Philippians 4:13)

9. **Prayer**: Lord, remind me that my failures do not define me. Help me to see myself through Your eyes, as a beloved child with a purpose.
Scripture: *"For we are God's handiwork, created in Christ Jesus to do good works, which God prepared in advance for us to do."* (Ephesians 2:10)

10.**Prayer**: Father, as I rise from failure, may I encourage others who are struggling. Let my testimony be a source of hope and inspiration.
Scripture: *"Praise be to the God and Father of our Lord Jesus Christ, the Father of compassion and the God of all comfort."* (2 Corinthians 1:3)

Dear Kingdom Full Tabernacle International Ministries Family,

We want to extend our heartfelt gratitude to each and every one of you for participating in this year's 21-day fast. It has truly been an incredible time, as we united in prayer four times a day with hundreds of thousands of believers from across the globe. The power of God was evident as we gathered, and we have been truly blessed by the overwhelming testimonies of miracles, signs, and wonders that followed our prayers. It is inspiring to see how faithful God is, and we give Him all the glory for the breakthroughs that have come forth.

We encourage you to stay connected with us as we continue this journey of faith. We are present on Facebook, Instagram, TikTok, Twitter, and YouTube, and we even have a podcast to keep you spiritually nourished throughout the year. As you remain plugged in, remember the words of 2 Timothy 4:5: "*But you, be sober in all things, endure hardship, do the work of an evangelist, fulfill your ministry.*" Continue to share what God has done and is doing with those around you. Whether you join us in person or online, stay engaged with what God is doing here at Kingdom Full Tabernacle!

As you press forward, remember that we serve a victorious God. His word declares in 1 Corinthians 15:57, "*But thanks be to God, who gives us the victory through our Lord Jesus Christ.*" You are already victorious in Christ, and we stand on the promise of Romans 8:37: "*No, in all these things we are more than conquerors through him who loved us.*" Keep these scriptures close as a reminder that every challenge we face has already been overcome by the power of God.

However, it is important to be aware that after a season of fasting and spiritual breakthroughs, temptations may arise, just as they did for Jesus after His 40-day fast (Matthew 4:1-11). The enemy often seeks to distract and discourage us after such powerful encounters with God. You may face temptations of doubt, complacency, or even physical and emotional challenges, but remember, Jesus responded to every temptation with the Word of God. Stay rooted in the Word and in prayer as you guard the spiritual gains you've made.

It's also crucial to remain consistent in the habits and disciplines you developed during this fast. Galatians 6:9 reminds us, *"Let us not become weary in doing good, for at the proper time we will reap a harvest if we do not give up."* Trust that God is faithful to answer every prayer, though the timing may not always be immediate. Stay committed to what God has instructed you during this time, and continue to believe that He is working behind the scenes to bring every promise to fulfillment.

Thank you again for joining us on this spiritual journey. We look forward to seeing what God will continue to do in your life and in the life of our ministry. Stay blessed, stay connected, and stay victorious!

With love, gratitude, and courage,

Apostle Dominic Osei, MDiv
Prophetess Lesley Osei, MS
Kingdom Full Tabernacle International Ministries

Made in United States
Orlando, FL
08 November 2024